Osprey Modelling • 18

Modelling the Marder
Self-Propelled Gun

Sam Dwyer

Consultant editor Robert Oehler
Series editors Marcus Cowper and Nikolai Bogdanovic

First published in Great Britain in 2005 by Osprey Publishing
Midland House, West Way, Botley, Oxford OX2 0PH, UK
443 Park Avenue South, New York, NY 10016, USA
Email: info@ospreypublishing.com

ISBN 1 84176 855 3

Page layout by Servis Filmsetting Ltd, Manchester, UK
Index by Alison Worthington
Originated by Solidity Graphics, London, UK
Printed and bound in China through Bookbuilders

05 06 07 08 09   10 9 8 7 6 5 4 3 2 1

A CIP catalogue record for this book is available from the British Library.

For a catalogue of all books published by Osprey Military
and Aviation please contact:

NORTH AMERICA
Osprey Direct, 2427 Bond Street, Univeristy Park, IL 60466, USA
E-mail: info@ospreydirectusa.com

ALL OTHER REGIONS
Osprey Direct UK, P.O. Box 140, Wellingborough, Northants, NN8 2FA, UK
E-mail: info@ospreydirect.co.uk

www.ospreypublishing.com

Acknowledgements

While it is my name on the front cover of this book, there are many people who in their own way helped, contributed, cajoled, bullied, and encouraged me through the entire process. I'd like to give special mention to the following people: Anthony Sheedy for his assistance with the Marder II, and for being my sounding board with all the builds in this book. Andrew Dextras, James Blackwell, Graeme Davidson, Nick Cortese, and Mic Bradshaw for all their support as well. To the generous suppliers whom contributed – Peter Kwok at K59, Waclaw Peszko at Aber, Roberto Reale at Royal Model, and Joe Bakanovic III at Tiger Model Designs – thanks guys. Finally, I want to dedicate this book to Rae, Eleanor, and Patrick. Thanks guys.

Sam Dwyer, November 2004.

Contents

Introduction

A little history

As a by-product of having conquered many European countries from 1938 to 1940, including Czechoslovakia, Germany found herself in possession of some very modern tanks and tank production facilities. Tanks produced by the CKD Werke in Czechoslovakia, the 35(t) and 38(t), were used in great numbers by the Wehrmacht during the war. When these became obsolete on the battlefield, they were converted into tank destroyers, or *panzerjägers* (literally – 'tank hunters') by fitting a potent anti-tank gun to an open fighting compartment. Germany captured hundreds of Russian 7.62cm anti-tank guns, an extremely powerful weapon. They were mated to the Panzer II Ausf. D chassis, to form the Marder II Ausf. D. These were also fitted to the 38(t) chassis, to form the Panzerjäger 38(t) für 7.62cm PaK36(r) (Sd.Kfz.139). At the same time the Panzer IIc Ausf. A, B C and F were being phased out of service, the deadly PaK 40 75mm anti-tank gun was mated to this chassis to form the 7.5cm PaK40/2 auf Fahrgestell Panzer-kampfwagen II (Sf) (Sd.Kfz.131 Marder II. The German-produced PaK (*Panzer abwehr Kanone*) 40 was also mated to the Czech 38(t) chassis to form both the Marder III Ausf. H (7.5cm PaK40/3 auf Panzerkampfwagen 38(t), and the Marder III Ausf. M (Panzerjäger 38(t) mit PaK40/3 Ausf. M Sd.Kfz.138)

When I sat down to write this book, I was unsure what exactly to cover, Marders I, II or III? 1/72 scale or 1/35 scale? Should I concentrate on as many as possible, covering the whole family of vehicles? I was able to source an Ironside Marder I from eBay, so this was a logical inclusion and a good starter for the book. Alan Hobbies from the Ukraine popped up on the hobby radar in the late 1990s and amongst their releases was the Marder II Ausf. D. This kit is quite good, but the detail is a little heavy, and not up to the standard of releases from the likes of Tamiya. This of course makes it a perfect candidate for updating and reworking. In 2001 and 2002 Tamiya released two exquisite models, the Sd.Kfz. 138 Marder III(r) and the Sd.Kfz.138 Marder III Ausf. M. I couldn't write a book about modelling the Marder without including these fantastic kits, as they represent the pinnacle of injection moulding and ease of construction. In 1973 Italeri released a Marder III Ausf. H. This was based on their 38(t) kit. For its time it was a great model with great detail and, up until the Tamiya releases, was still deemed to be very detailed. I believe it to still be one of Italeri's best releases.

This book starts off assuming the reader understands the basics of armour modelling, construction, painting, and decaling. Hence I've not included any 'out of the box' builds. While all the kits above can be built out of the box quite well, each subject also benefits from detail improvements. I've also kept basic construction in progress pictures to a minimum, concentrating instead on highlighting new techniques in photographs and descriptions. Each chapter adds another skill, culminating in the final chapter where I bring everything covered previously together to produce a super-detailed diorama.

Tools and materials

I always find any discussion on tools and materials that individual modeller uses very interesting. What one modeller swears by, the next modeller may shun as a useless extravagance. There are some items in a modeller's toolbox that every modeller will use:

- Modelling/craft knife. Self-explanatory. Also you'll need a large supply of no. 11 straight, curved, and chisel blades. I seem to break the tip off the straight blades at a phenomenal rate. Once the blades are a little dull, I just use them for applying superglue and putty.

- Glue – I use Tamiya super-thin liquid plastic cement and Testors' liquid plastic cement.
- Cyanoacrylate glue (CA) or 'superglue'. There are a million different brands and viscosities available, though I tend to stick with Selley's Supa-glue, and Tamiya non-fogging CA.
- Putty – I use Tamiya grey putty, and occasionally Squadron green. I also use Miliput and Epoxie Sculpt two-part epoxy putty.
- Files – I picked up a pack of 10 different diamond files very cheaply at a train show many years ago, they still show no signs of wearing out or clogging.
- Glass fibre sanding pen. Literally made up of thousands of fine glass fibres, perfect for sanding and smoothing hard to reach areas.
- Paint – an obvious inclusion, but one that stirs great emotion in many modellers. Some are die-hard enamel users (Humbrol), and a growing number use exclusively acrylics (Tamiya, Gunze, Vallejo just to name a few). I almost solely use Tamiya acrylics, but for this book I will use Gunze and Vallejo as well.
- Brushes – both fine point and broad. Used for applying glue, putty, paint, and pastels.
- Punch and die set – Historex, both round and Hex – not cheap, but a one-off purchase that will last a modeller a lifetime.
- Pyrogravure – a soldering iron-like tool for replicating weld seams, available through Historex Agents. Once again, not cheap, but a one-off investment.
- Airbrush – I use two: a Tamiya Superfine HG and an Iwata Custom Micron. A good airbrush is again a one-off purchase and, treated well, will last forever.
- Air compressor – for running your airbrush. Self-explanatory.
- Pliers and side cutters – I use pliers to bend photo-etched brass. These pliers meet perfectly, and have a right angle on them. Beats paying large sums for dedicated etch benders. Side cutters are perfect for removing parts from the sprues. The ones I use are German, designed for use in electronics manufacture. These are a little expensive, but worth every penny, considering you will use these with every model.
- Pin vice and drill bits – for drilling tiny holes in things. Also, by chuckling a pin in your pin vice, it's a great tool for marking and scribing panel lines.
- A dedicated model room – many modellers take a dedicated space to build and paint models for granted. Up until the birth of my now two-year-old twins, I had my own model room, with built in wardrobes full of bookshelves and kit storage. For a spell I worked off the kitchen table, taking photographs of my models on a TV stand set up in the laundry. Now I have a space set aside in the garage, the spiders don't seem to mind the smell of paint and glue fumes. Along with this it pays to have as much light and ventilation in your model room as possible – it's meant to be a hobby, so going blind from working in the dark or choking on glue or paint fumes is something to avoid!
- Tamiya Panzer IV OVM – basically the tool sprue from Tamiya's excellent Panzer IV Ausf. H and J. Sold separately, invaluable for upgrading the tool stowage on older kits.

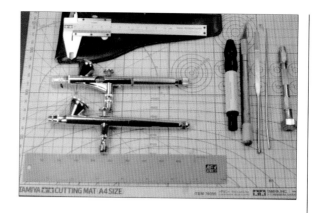

ABOVE, TOP Tools of the trade. The Tamiya precision caliper is required for accurate measuring. The pin vice, X-acto knife and glass fibre stick are for drilling, cutting and sanding respectively. Probably the most expensive modelling tool you'll ever buy is an airbrush, but if it is maintained well it should last a modelling lifetime.

ABOVE A selection of the paints used in the book. Virtually all paint manufacturers have their own take on German World War II camouflage colours. A cross-section of paints was used on each model, dispelling the myth that enamels and acrylics can't be used in conjunction on the same model.

Sd.Kfz.135 Marder I

Subject:	*7.5cm PaK40/1 auf Geschutzwagen Lorraine Schlepper(f), Sd.Kfz.135 Marder I*
Skill Level:	*Intermediate*
Base Kit:	*Ironside Marder 1*
Scale:	*1/35*
Additional detailing sets used:	*AFV Club PaK 40 (AF35071)*
	AFV Club PaK 40 ammunition (AF35075)
	Friulmodel Marder I/Lorraine Schlepper track

History

During and after the fall of France in 1940, the German Army captured massive quantities of French armour, much of it virtually undamaged. Forever looking for new chassis to mount anti-tank guns on, the Wehrmacht converted 170 French 'Tracteur Blindé 37L (Lorraine)' by adding the powerful Rheinmetall-Borsig produced PaK 40 75mm anti-tank gun. This combination was known as the '7.5cm PaK40/1 auf Geschützwagen Lorraine Schlepper(f), Sd.Kfz.135'. This vehicle was also known as the Marder I. An interesting aside is that the conversion of these vehicles was arranged by Captain Alfred Becker, commander of Stug. Abt. 200. Becker used his pre-war business contacts to have these vehicles converted in both France and Krefeld, Germany. These vehicles were originally assigned to units fighting on the Eastern Front, but were returned to France in 1943 to equip units serving in the occupation force. With only armour protection against small arms and shell fragments, these thin-skinned, open-topped vehicles could hardly slug it out with Allied armour, but were very effective on the defensive, perfectly suited to the fighting in the bocage country of Normandy.

The model

I searched high and low for a kit of the Marder I, but initially to no avail. There have however been a few full kits of it produced over the years, the oldest probably being the MB Models release in resin and photo-etch. However, I've not seen it generally available for at least eight or nine years. AlBy of France released perhaps the best kit of the Marder I, also in resin, but I've never seen one of these even more elusive rarities in the flesh either. RPM of Russia had a Marder I in their catalogue, along with the straight Lorraine Schlepper towing a PaK 40, but finding either of these kits also proved tricky. Plastic model companies in the former Soviet Union seem to pop up and disappear every day of the week, and of course when I want one of their kits, none are available. I turned to eBay in desperation, and after only a week or two of searching, I came across the last option I know of, produced by the French company Azimut's plastic kit offshoot Ironside. Six days later the kit was winging its way to my door. This kit contained a bonus, a set of Friulmodellismo white metal workable track links.

This kit hardly represents the pinnacle of injection-moulding technology. It doesn't even represent the pinnacle of limited-run injection-moulding technology. Released sometime in the 1990s, it comprises five sprues of soft grey plastic, a resin transmission, a turned aluminium barrel, and a small sheet of photo-etched brass. This brass, even after repeatedly being heated and allowed to cool (annealed), remained stiff and unworkable. Being a limited-run injection-

Sd Kfz 135/1 7,5 cm PAK auf Gw Lorraine MARDE
1/3

AZIMUT
PRODUCTIONS

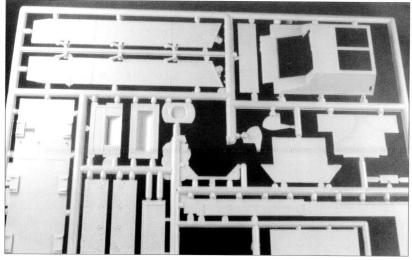

ABOVE The Ironside Marder I
box art.

LEFT Kit sprues. As you can see,
very heavy sprue gates and flash
between parts.

moulded kit, the sprue gates are heavy, the detail is fairly heavy and poor, and it
just cries out to be detailed!

Construction

While the purpose of this book isn't to discuss the basic construction of any
model, I feel that there needs to be some discussion of the techniques used
while building these limited-run kits. I've found that the best approach to
getting the kit right is to get all the parts square, i.e. all the mating surfaces, or
surfaces to be glued together, nice and straight. Errors in construction tend to

compound, ending in a model that doesn't sit flat on the table or base. If some time is spent early in the construction process in getting things square, the final product turns out much better.

Once the hull tub has been cleaned of all the flash and assembled, it can be set aside for the glue to harden fully. This is really important, as the plastic used in Ironside kits tends to stay soft long after liquid glue has been applied. I sped up the process by using Cyanoacrylate to harden and strengthen the bonds.

I found that the forward upper armour wasn't long enough, and left a 2mm gap between the front and rear upper sections. I filled this gap with Evergreen plastic rectangle-section rod. Glue the rods on too long and trim the excess when the glue is dry. I aligned the outer edge of the rod with the outside of the hull to save on filling later.

Bring all the hull sections together, checking for gaps. There are always gaps, and this is one of the reasons I love armour modelling – there are *meant* to be gaps! Still, gaps on a model of this scale need to 35 times smaller than the corresponding gaps on the real vehicle, so it's out with the Mr Surfacer 500. This liquid putty finds it own level, settles into gaps, and sands well. I brush it on carefully, let it do its thing, and sand if necessary.

One of the first things you notice with these vehicles is the relative thinness of the armour. The armour on the Marder family is only really meant to protect the crew from shell splinters and small-arms fire. As I've mentioned previously, Marders weren't designed to slug it out with tanks and tank destroyers, though that would have been of little comfort to their vulnerable crews. However the Ironside kit comes with one-piece upper side armour plates, with heavy engraved grooves on the inside to facilitate bending the plates into the correct shape. The first thing I noticed here is how unbelievably thick this plastic is – it looked like battleship armour! So I started off by replacing the lower side armour plates.

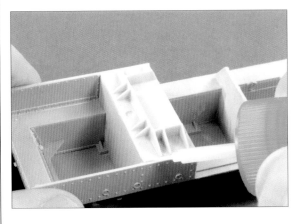

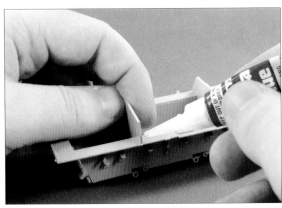

Applying Tamiya super thin glue. Capillary action draws the glue between the parts. I strengthened joins using CA glue for a permanent bond

These plates aren't just flat plates, they both (left and right side) have a large air vent cut into them. At this stage of construction, I opted to leave out the louvres as they were bound to get damaged later on. I used the kit parts as a template here to get the vent location right. That's why this is such a great subject for an introduction to scratch-building, it's all just flat plates. I used Evergreen .015in. plastic card, as .010in. card tended to warp. I placed angled spacers inside the angled hull armour to provide and maintain the correct angle of these lower plates.

The upper armour was again copied from the kit parts. I copied one part onto plastic card, and then made another copy using the plastic card master. This is pure monkey work, but it pays to spend some time and effort getting these parts the same and the edges square. The upper armour wasn't glued to the hull at this stage, as I still needed to detail the inner surfaces and paint them. One of the hardest things to do is paint an open-topped vehicle with the sides glued in place!

One of the worst aspects of this kit is unfortunately the gun. In terms of construction, this Marder I was built last, after all the other models in this book. The reason for this was that I had discovered the Taiwanese company AFV Club was about to release a brand new PaK 40. The second it was available, I knew I had to use it on this kit.

This kit, unlike the Ironside Marder I, really is a work of art. Within 40 minutes of it arriving, I had the gun parts assembled. No flash, perfect fit of parts, great detail – it's all there. The gun cradle assembly on the real

Marder I consisted of the basic PaK 40, minus the gun trail and with a new gun shield. I started to graft the PaK 40 to the Ironside kit by modifying the lower trail mount. I cut off the rear trail mounts, and added mounting hardware from Evergreen card together with bolts from the punch and die set.

The new front gun shield was copied from the kit part, traced onto .015in. plastic card. The hinges from the kit part were cut out and were detailed with rivets from the punch and die set. This gun shield differs from the standard PaK 40 gun shield; I sadly couldn't use the beautiful stamped-brass two-piece spaced armour shield that comes in the AFV Club kit. Into the spares box it went, it's just too good not to use on something later on! The shield on the Marder I has hinged edges; the only possible explanation for this is to allow for extended traverse for the gun. The new plastic card gun shield just glues onto the mounts for the shield on the PaK 40 gun mount. I left the gun separate, as, once again, it's virtually impossible to paint this properly if glued into the hull.

Pictures of a surviving example of a Marder I at the Saumur tank museum in France show evidence of a tread plate floor on the same level as the lower part of the under-gun ammo rack. There are clamps and brackets here; I made the assumption that the Germans added this floor when the original Lorraine chassis was remanufactured into a Marder. Therefore I added a 'dot pattern' tread plate floor. I also added the under-gun ammo rack, thinning the kit parts heavily, then re-drilling the holes, to allow Tamiya turned-brass ammo to fit snugly. I'm not sure what the designers were thinking when they added an ammo rack *under* the main armament – the gunner and loader would be tripping over each other in an engagement!

There is some conjecture as to where the radio mount is located in the Marder I. The sole (as far as I'm aware) surviving example of Marder I shows some evidence of radio installation in the front right corner of the superstructure. There are small clips along the inside of the right upper armour, indicating that a wiring conduit ran from the front right corner to the rear right corner, where the antenna mount was located. With this in mind, I started building a mount, and a radio. I was able to source a leftover radio from the Tamiya Marder III Ausf. M. The mount I surmised is similar to the mount in the Wespe, in fact most radio mounts in German open-topped self-propelled guns are similar. They consist of the radio receiver set itself, a power transformer, and a junction box (for switching between vehicle intercom and platoon/ company/battalion nets).

The radio itself was detailed with a brass wire grab handle and a shockproof rack, which was then glued into the hull corner. All the associated wiring and hardware was added as per the photographs. The transformer, intercom boxes, and antenna boot are castings of parts I've modified from parts available in other kits.

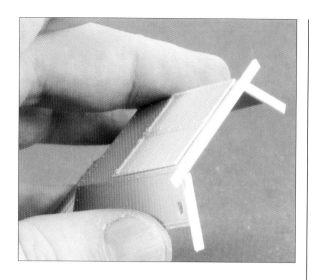

Nasty gap – easy fix. Evergreen styrene rod glues easily and is a quick gap filler.

Brushing on Mr Surfacer with an old brush. The best way to apply this is to allow the putty to flow into the gaps and find its own level. This minimizes sanding later.

Adding the lower additional armour. As with the real vehicle, the armour plate was added directly over the existing vehicle armour. .015in. Evergreen styrene was used.

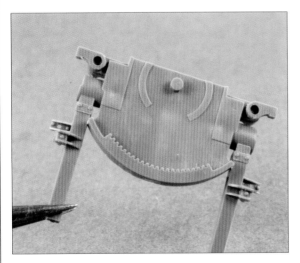

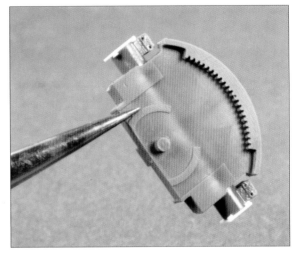

ABOVE, ABOVE RIGHT AND
RIGHT The AFV Club gun mount;
it's just a matter of trimming off the
trail attachment points, adding
mounting plates from styrene, and
gluing to the Ironside hull. Note
the tiny securing bolts.

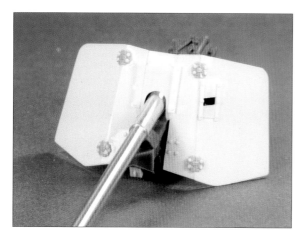

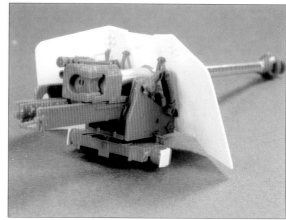

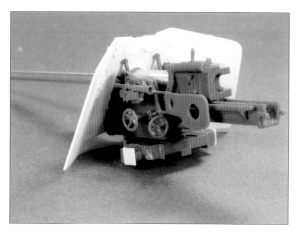

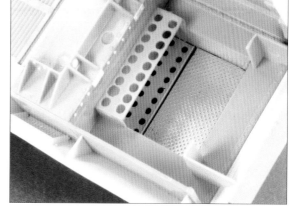

TOP LEFT, TOP RIGHT AND ABOVE The completed, unpainted gun and mantlet. .015in. Evergreen was used to fashion the shield. Hinges from the Ironside kit were carefully sanded off and glued to the new gun shield. You can tell the AFV Club gun is great, no styrene was added!

ABOVE New 'dot pattern' tread plate floor. This was added from now unavailable On the Mark Models photo-etched tread plate.

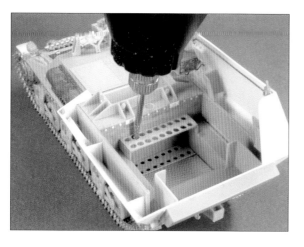

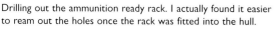

Drilling out the ammunition ready rack. I actually found it easier to ream out the holes once the rack was fitted into the hull.

Fitting the turned brass Tamiya PaK 40 ammo. In reality, this late in the war, steel cases were substituted for brass, but these were just too nice to paint over!

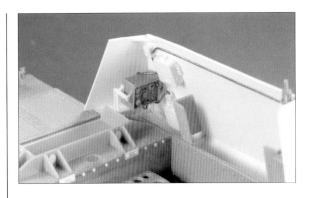

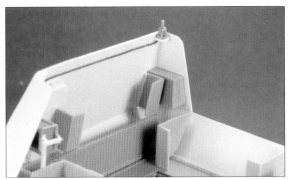

ABOVE Radio and installation. The radio came from the Tamiya Marder III Ausf. M, the wiring is fine solder and brass wire.

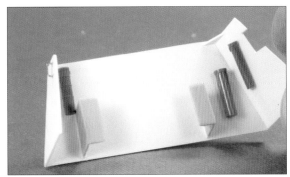

ABOVE RIGHT AND RIGHT Fighting compartment interior. The Marder I had quite a spartan interior compared to others in the family, indicative of being a stopgap solution.

Along with the lower side armour plates, the upper plates were copied using the original kit parts as templates. Again, .015in. Evergreen plastic card was used to avoid warpage common to the thinner gauges of plastic card. These upper hull sides were detailed according to the excellent *Panzers in Saumur* photo journal. Brush bins (containers holding the gun cleaning brushes) and various stowage boxes were added. The side ammo racks in the Marder I are a very basic affair, literally being bent pieces of metal designed to hold pressed-steel PaK 40 ammunition shipping containers. I used the Ironside kit parts here, thinned heavily.

As is common with a lot of Eastern Bloc kits, or limited-run injection-moulded kits, detail on some parts isn't as good as it possibly could be. This is highlighted by the vehicle tools – axe heads, shovels, jack, headlights, and horns. I mentioned in the 'Tools and equipment' section at the start of the book that Tamiya have released the tool sprue from their excellent Panzer IV Ausf. J. This is an absolute godsend for kits like the Ironside Marder I. The jack, horn, and Notek blackout light from the kit were dropped in favour of the corresponding parts from the Panzer IV tool set. These items alone really lift the tone of the vehicle.

On the front of the vehicle, I replaced the fenders with ones made from Evergreen styrene sheet. The kit contains fenders in photo-etched brass, but I found these to be totally unworkable, even after annealing. Rivets were added to the fenders from Grandt Line no. 153 domed rivets. These rivets were also added to the large photo-etched driver's hatch plates. The kit instructions advise the use of flat photo-etched hinges for this hatch, I replaced them with Evergreen strip, and the hinge section itself is .010in. lead wire. Next I replaced the kit's gun travel lock. The kit parts were thick and the detail basic, but was easily redone with Evergreen strip. The kit's travel lock mounts were thinned down, rivet mounting detail added, and then the whole section was glued to the upper hull front. Finally the etched exhaust cover was added – I annealed this about four times, nothing would remove the part's springiness. I overcame this by bending and dinging the cover. These parts were made of flimsy steel in real life.

Tools and jack mounts. Note the fine detail on the Tamiya jack. A marked improvement on the part supplied in the Ironside kit.

Front vehicle tool stowage. Small steel pegs were welded to the final drive housing to mount the tow cable. Note the fine rivets added to the fenders and the dinged exhaust guard.

The first step in painting an open-topped vehicle like the Marder I is to assess which areas one can't get to once the sides are glued on. In this case, I painted the inside fighting compartment walls with a mix of Gunze H66 Sandy Brown and H11 Flat White. This paint is acrylic, and airbrushes very well through the Tamiya Superfine HG airbrush. It dries with a slight sheen, perfect for decaling and weathering. Care was taken to cover all the grey kit plastic, Evergreen white plastic, AFV Club's green plastic, and etched brass.

It's at this point while painting a model that I tend to think 'urgh!' The basic colour invariably to my eyes looks drab and awful. I feel that careful weathering is what lifts an average model to a showstopper. The first step, after airbrushing the basic colour is to pick out all the minor details: things like radios and intercom boxes. I used Humbrol 85 Coal Black and a fine brush. Most internal components of German AFVs were painted a satin black colour, and this Humbrol colour is perfect. The FuG radio itself was painted Humbrol 111 Field Grey. These items were painted in at this stage, prior to weathering, as they would of course weather and wear at the same rate as the rest of the interior.

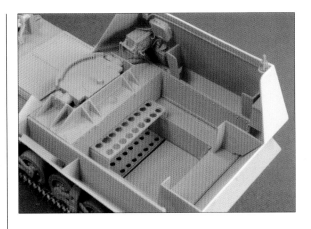

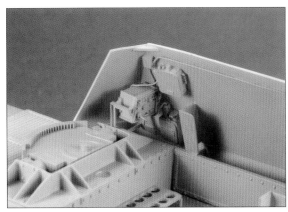

ABOVE AND ABOVE RIGHT Finally some paint added. Gunze paint sprays beautifully. All the different coloured plastic used in construction is covered and the kit is starting to look good.

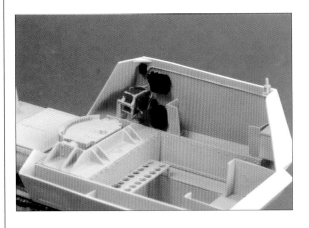

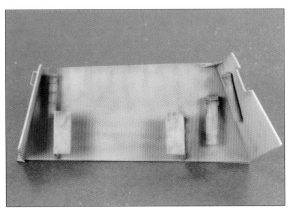

All the small details like radios painted in. The interior isn't looking so bare now. The stark paint is just crying out to be dirtied up!

Effects of a careful post shade application. See how the paint has been made to look more grubby and lived in. Horizontal streaks were added where the ammo would bump and scrape against the outer armour.

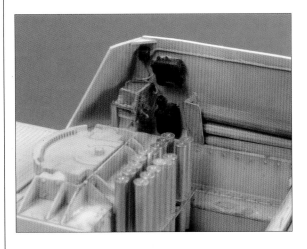

ABOVE AND ABOVE RIGHT Now the interior is looking more realistic. Pastel chalk has been applied to the walls and floor and paint chips added with a lead pencil. Dirty boot prints have been added just to personalize the interior. Note the ammo canisters.

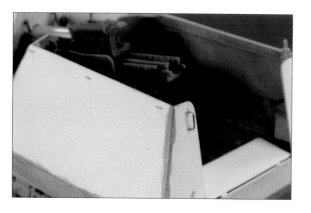

Now the upper armour plates can be glued to the hull permanently. Welds have been blended with Mr Surfacer.

Finished model ready for paint. Note the size of the PaK 40 in relation to the rest of the vehicle. The Marder I was tiny!

Once all the paint was completely dry I applied a thin 'wash' to the fighting compartment interior. This process has been referred to as many different things over the years, but at the end of the day, its just applying a thin 'glaze' of oil paint over the base coat. I made up a mix of turpentine and Humbrol 33 Matt Black paint, and applied it with a large flat brush evenly over the inner surfaces and floor of the fighting compartment. Once dry, the tint settles into and around detail, accentuating it and adding visual interest. The next step is to apply a post shade. James Blackwell developed this much talked-about technique. Post shading can only effectively be achieved with the use of a good airbrush; I used my Iwata CM-B Custom Micron. I mixed up some Tamiya acrylic thinners with a drop of Tamiya XF64 Red Brown and two or three drops of Tamiya XF1 Matt Black. This was then airbrushed around detail and, like the wash procedure, is used to highlight and define detail.

The next step in weathering the interior of the Marder I is to apply pastel chalks to simulate dust. I tend to like the interior of my open-topped vehicles to be dusty and dingy, and to show signs of being lived in. I grind up a cheap, light sand-coloured pastel chalk on some very rough sand paper, leaving me with a neat pile of pastel dust. This gets liberally applied into corners, nooks and crannies – anywhere dirt and grime would gather and not be worn away by human traffic. I use a combination of chisel-shaped brushes, round pointed ones, broad flat ones, and old scraggy brushes. The effect I'm trying to achieve is one of random dust and paint wear. Once this is done the next step is to add paint chips. This is quite a controversial subject – some modellers swear that paint needs to be chipped to make wear look realistic, others swear that this effect is unnecessary as German vehicles in late World War II didn't have the life span needed for the paint to chip. Anyway, I use a Derwent black pencil, and a 2B clutch pencil to add paint chips – the Derwent to simulate older chips, where the revealed metal has tarnished and turned black, and the 2B to simulate new chips. These chips are added to areas of high wear – edges, bolts, handles etc. Ammo stowage is added using Tamiya turned-brass PaK 40 ammunition for the under-gun ready-rack, and AFV Club's PaK 40 ammunition packing tubes for the side and rear lockers. This was weathered along the same lines as the rest of the interior.

Now that the interior of the fighting compartment is weathered, the sides can be glued on, the gaps filled, and weld beads added to the external armour plate. These welds were added with a pyrogravure – essentially a miniature fine-tipped soldering iron. It melts the plastic and, when used in a jabbing motion, is great for forming continuous weld beads. These welds were given a light coat of Mr Surfacer 1000, just to blend them into the surrounding armour plate. I added a small grab handle to the rear plate, and three small tie-down loops to each upper hull side armour. These etched tie downs were sourced from a leftover Aber set.

Painting

I've only ever come across a handful of pictures of Marder Is in service, and fewer still in use in Normandy. The few I have seen show them sporting a soft mottled camouflage scheme of green and brown over a dark yellow base coat. To kick this off I misted on three light coats of the same paint mix I used on the interior. Once dry, I applied the camouflage pattern of Gunze H406 Chocolate Brown and Gunze H405 Olive Green. Gunze paints airbrush beautifully, covering well and not spattering at all. Only basic markings seemed to have been applied to Normandy Marder Is – I've seen examples with large three-digit numbers, and some with only *balkenkreuz* (plain black and white crosses). These were added to the hull sides; at this stage I also painted the tyres with Humbrol Matt Black. The tyres were only roughly painted in, each wheel has a raised lip that would be worn silver as the vehicle moved – I highlighted this feature with 2B pencil – more on that later. After leaving the decals to dry for an hour or two, I coated the entire vehicle with Humbrol Matt Coat. This gives the vehicle an all over dead matt finish. The next step is to apply a post shade coat to the entire vehicle. I applied a particularly heavy coat to the tow cable and the run of spare track mounted on the front of the vehicle.

Weathering

The battle for Normandy was fought in the height of summer; this is reflected in period photographs – vehicles, markings and camouflage patterns obscured by dust. With this in mind I set about applying pastels to the model. Achieving the right balance between a realistic finish and a 'pastel bomb' is often tricky; the key I think is restraint. I used a mix of light pink, and the same light sand colour I used on the interior. I applied pastels randomly to the lower hull and running gear quite heavily, adding pastels less heavily further up the hull.

BELOW AND NEXT PAGE The model painted. This is just the basic camouflage colours, and decals. All small details like tyres and tools have been painted in preparation for weathering.

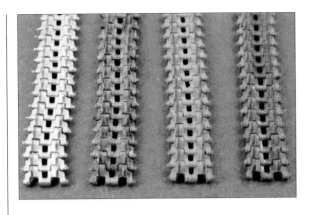

Friulmodellisimo white metal tracks, and the four steps to weathering. The tracks are white bright metal when new, careful weathering really brings out the detail and enhances realism.

Tracks mounted on the vehicle. The edges of the links are metalled up with a lead pencil.

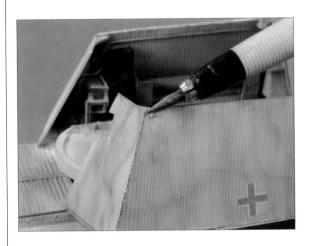

Final step before completion – add some minor paint chips to the edges of the armour plate with a lead pencil.

ABOVE AND PAGES 19–20 **Views of the finished model.**

At this stage, I built and painted the tracks. The tracks that come in the kit are horrific. They're poorly moulded and virtually impossible to put together. Friulmodellisimo of Italy has released a white metal set of replacement track. These tracks are workable – not so that you can push the kit along the floor, but so that between return rollers, the tracks sag realistically. As these track links are metal, I applied a blackening solution to the links. This, as its name suggests, blackens or patinas the track, kicking off the weathering process. The next step is to apply a slurry of pastel chalk and Tamiya acrylic thinner to the tracks. Once dry, I 'metalled' the links, adding a wear pattern with a 2B pencil.

As a final touch on the Marder I, before the gun and mantlet was permanently attached to the hull, I added chips and wear to the top edges of the armour plate. This is the area the crew would logically hang on to when traversing rough ground. The top edge of the armour plate would wear and chip; I applied these chips again with a 2B pencil and a Derwent black pencil.

The final step is to weather the PaK 40 gun and shield. The gun was heavily chipped and stained with dark brown and black pastel chalk – the grimier the better. The gun really is the centrepiece of this kit; therefore it received the most attention in the weathering process. The gun sight was painted with Humbrol 85 Coal Black, the gun was glued into the hull, and the kit was finished.

Sd.Kfz.132 Marder II Ausf. D

Subject:	Panzer Selbstfahrlafette 1 fur 7.62cm PaK36(r) auf Fahrgestell Panzerkampwagen II Ausf. D (Sd.Kfz.132) 'Marder II Ausf. D'
Skill Level:	Intermediate
Base Kit:	Alan Hobbies Marder II Ausf. D
Scale:	1/35
Additional detailing sets used:	Modelkasten workable tracks (SK56) Gun from Tamiya Marder III (MM35248) Tools from Tamiya Panzer IV OVM equipment set

History

The Marder II Ausf. D was based on the chassis of the Panzer II Ausf. D and E. The full designation of this Marder was quite a mouthful: Panzer Selbstfahr-lafette 1 für 7.62cm PaK36(r) auf Fahrgestell PzKpfw II, Ausf. D. This Marder II (there were in fact two Marder IIs: this one, and one armed with the PaK 40/2, based on the Panzer II Ausf. A, B, C and F chassis) was armed with a captured Soviet 76.2mm anti-tank gun, designated as 76.2mm PaK 36(r) L/51 anti-tank gun by the Germans, and rechambered to accept 75mm PaK 40 ammunition. Extending the height of the front and sides of the superstructure above the fender line, and adding a sturdy pedestal on which to mount the gun, created a basic fighting compartment. This resulted in a high silhouette. An extended gun shield provided the main protection for the four-man crew. It is believed that up to 30 rounds of ammunition was carried, but no vehicles survive to this day to verify the fact. In addition to the main gun, and as per standard practice for German open-topped self-propelled guns, a 7.92mm MG34 was carried inside the fighting compartment. Again, as with all German armour, improvements and variations were incorporated during production and by the troops in the field. Later versions had a wire mesh section added in place of the rear upper armour, along with a slight redesign in the gun shield. The gun shield was of virtually the same design as the shield on the Marder III, the difference was that the one on the Marder II was welded rather than riveted. The German tank manufacturing firms Alkett and Wegmann converted 201 vehicles from April 1942 to June 1943. Marder II Ausf. Ds served mainly on the Eastern Front from April 1942 onwards.

The model

This model of the Marder II Ausf. D was released by Russian company Alan Hobbies in 2001, and is typical of many Eastern European releases, featuring heavy mould lines, sprue gates, and fairly basic detail.

Construction

This of course makes it a fantastic candidate for freshening up. There are a couple of ways of going about this. One way would be to attend to every error or omission in the kit, using basic modelling and scratch-building skills, i.e. removing heavy mould lines, filling knock-out pin marks, and adding lots of details that aren't included in the basic kit. Another option is to replace the deficient parts of the Alan Hobbies kit with parts available in other kits, or parts

MARDER II D

СБОРНАЯ МОДЕЛЬ — КОПИЯ
САМОХОДНОГО ОРУДИЯ

214

alan   1/35 MILITARY MINIATURE SERIES NO 01

Alan Hobbies Marder II Ausf. D
box art.

from aftermarket manufacturers. I've chosen this method, as it yields the best results for the least amount of effort.

The first step here is to assess the kit parts, and determine what needs to be replaced or improved. Upon first glance, it's evident that the kit wheels aren't up to standard. The detail here is fairly poor and soft. ModelKasten have in their comprehensive range of working tracks kit SK-56, a set of replacement wheels and tracks for the Marder II. The wheels included in this set are a huge leap forward in detail over the kit-supplied wheels, and are an easy addition to the kit. While on the suspension, I detailed the drive sprocket with bolt heads taken from a spare Panther roadwheel, and filled a nasty sink mark in the centre of each sprocket.

The basic hull was built up as per kit instructions. I won't go over this, as by now everyone should how to know to glue things together! I will say that more care needs to be taken with kits of Eastern Bloc origin, they tend not to 'fall' together the way Tamiya, Dragon, or AFV Club kits do. Not to say that they are bad, but it just takes some more effort for the same reward. Typical of many Eastern Bloc kits, the hull comprises four parts, where one would have sufficed. That said, the hull went together with no problems. I wanted to make sure I had a good base before I began detailing the hull, so I ensured all the hull joins were solid, neat, and dry before starting some basic detailing. As mentioned in the previous chapter, Tamiya have released a set of generic German tools that are perfect for detailing virtually any German World War II armoured vehicle. First step is to add or replace all the tool stowage, and the lights and horn. The Tamiya parts are exquisite, as can be seen in the accompanying photos.

The hull interior of the Marder II Ausf. D is one of those mysteries in German armour modelling circles that ranks up there with who shot JKF and Area 51 – there is just so much conjecture as to how this area was configured

Basic hull construction. The hull of the Marder II Ausf. D is very boxy, typical of Marders. The armour plates are commendably thin in the Alan Hobbies kit. Note the brown ModelKasten wheels.

Adding rivets to the drive sprockets. The large grey area in the centre of the rivets is Tamiya putty, covering a large sink hole.

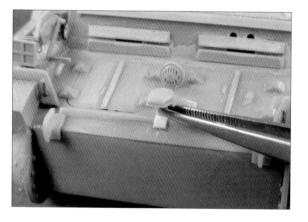

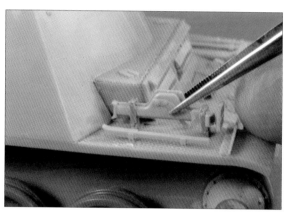

ABOVE AND ABOVE RIGHT Adding tools and vehicle stowage, from the Tamiya Panzer IV tool set. This set is a must have when working with kits of Eastern European origin.

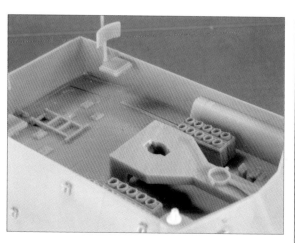

ABOVE AND ABOVE RIGHT Fighting compartment interior. There isn't a lot of information as to the configuration of the Marder II Ausf. D interior.

Gun muzzle brake. I detailed the muzzle with tiny plastic rings on the inside, and a small lock nut and strip on the outside.

it's not funny. Rather than develop my own interpretation of how this area was set up, which would be outside the scope of the build, I chose to rather refine what Alan Hobbies suggest the interior should look like. I replaced the vertical ammo stowage with racks taken from the Tamiya Marder III. I ordered the individual ammo rack (and gun – more on that later) sprues from Rainbow 10, a mail order model store in Japan. Ordering sprues like this saves destroying an entire kit just for parts. I trimmed the Tamiya vertical ammo racks to fit in the gaps on the fighting compartment floor. The horizontal ammo racks came from the spares box. The antenna base is a resin casting I made from a Tamiya master many years ago. The crew seats, gun travel locks and gun pedestal were added as per kit instructions. Unfortunately, there is just not enough information on this area to embellish the detail further.

Moving onto the gun, it was an easy choice to replace the whole assembly with the gun from the Tamiya Marder III (kit number 35248). As mentioned above, I purchased the whole gun sprue from Rainbow 10. It's possibly the quickest and easiest way of improving the detail of this kit. The Tamiya parts were built virtually out of the box, with a few exceptions. I detailed the muzzle brake with Evergreen plastic card rings, made with the punch and die, and plastic locking strip. Also, the gun shield on the Marder II seems to have been of welded construction, so the rivets were carefully shaved off the Tamiya parts (and saved for later), and weld detail was added in their place. I added this

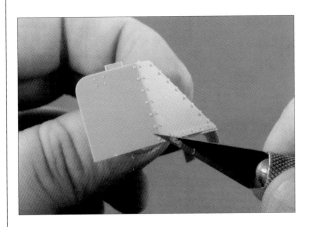

Begin by scraping off all the moulded-on rivets.

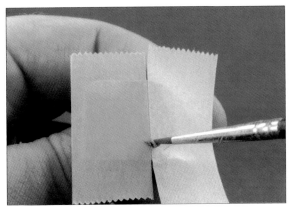

Tape off the area as a mask, then apply Tamiya putty with a brush. I textured the putty while still wet with the brush as well.

Once dry, the tape can be removed to reveal subtle weld details.

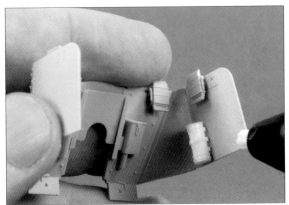

Sanding off the knock-out pin marks. I used a glass fibre pen available from electronics supply stores.

detail by firstly taping off the area with yellow Tamiya tape. As you can see I've left a tiny gap between the two pieces of tape. Onto this area I applied Tamiya putty with a brush, stippling it on in a rough manner. Once the putty was dry I removed the tape to reveal a perfectly neat weld seam. This detail was added to the external and internal faces of the gun shield. While I was working on the gun shield, I removed all knock-out punch marks from the inside face, and added gas mask containers.

At this stage I always fit the tracks to see if I have all the wheels lined up correctly. Don't laugh; it's a common thing to see a well-constructed model with wheels lined up crookedly. This is a very quick and easy build, thankfully, so we can now concentrate on the fun stuff – painting a worn winter white-wash camouflage. I always check now, before painting, that all gaps have been filled, and that I've not forgotten anything.

It's always a very satisfying feeling getting paint on a model; it's what I love the most about this hobby – the chance to express your artistic side. I wanted to depict this Marder at the end of winter, the whitewash camouflage worn and scraggy, and the tracks and wheels full of mud.

Painting

The first step is to apply a base coat of German grey. As the proceeding coats of paint would be attacked heavily in the weathering process, I used lacquer-based paint. Tamiya Mini Sprays are lacquer and spray beautifully. I gently heated the can in a bowl of hot water for five minutes, and applied three or four light coats, until the colour built up on all surfaces. Once dry, the Tamiya lacquer has a slight sheen, perfect for the application of decals.

I chose to use Vallejo acrylic Flat White for my whitewash camouflage. It covers beautifully, brushes well, and it's quite easy to degrade in the weathering process. Applying the whitewash is simply a matter of dipping the brush into the Vallejo white, and scrubbing it onto the Marder in a relatively haphazard manner – the scruffier looking the better. At this point it doesn't

BELOW AND RIGHT The model after three light coats of Tamiya Mini Spray German Grey. This paint is in an aerosol can, I warmed the can in a bowl of warm water, the paint sprayed beautifully and covered well.

Applying the whitewash. There is no real magic to this, just apply as you see fit – I applied it in a patchy manner so that lots of grey was showing through.

The Marder whitewashed. Note the cross-hatched pattern on the gun barrel. If you squint, the white paint really breaks up the outline of the vehicle.

Scrub the paint with a toothbrush. Go as hard as you like, the more you scrub, the more grey paint you will reveal.

Now the whitewash is totally degraded. The vehicle is starting to look like it's seen a tough winter.

really matter how it looks, as long as it looks bad! Vallejo acrylic paint dries very quickly, so this process literally only takes a few minutes.

Now, it's time to take to the white paint with extreme prejudice. My weapon of choice here is an old toothbrush. I used a cream cleanser (Jif here in Australia) as an abrasive agent, and just scrubbed and scrubbed with the toothbrush until the white paint began to wear away. This is the reason why I chose to basecoat the model in lacquer, its extremely tough and hardwearing. It's doubtful if Tamiya or Gunze acrylics would stand up to this punishment. I actually approached this fairly carefully, you don't want to be so aggressive that you completely remove all the white. I guess it comes down to personal taste, but I left a fair amount of white paint, with grey showing through. The Marder should now start to look like it's seen a hard winter's service.

The German Army was often quite fastidious (particularly early on in the war) in regards to vehicle markings. There is lots of pictorial evidence of national cross markings, *balkenkreuz*, being taped or masked up when the white camouflage was applied, so as to protect the markings during the painting process. I chose to perform this step kind of backwards, as decals don't stand up too well to being taped over, they tend to pull off the model. So I masked off a circle on each side of the Marder, and sprayed some Tamiya German Grey, over which I applied a plain white *balkenkreuz* decal to each hull side once the paint was dry.

ABOVE Simple decals applied. I kept the markings few as I wanted to highlight the winter paint finish.

RIGHT Post shade applied. Note how the white paint is starting to look dirtier than before. I concentrated the post shade around areas of detail and the top edges of armour plate.

The whitewash camouflage was further weathered by post shading. As described in the previous chapter, this consists of an extremely thin mix of Tamiya acrylic thinners, Tamiya XF1 Matt Black, and XF64 Red Brown applied with the airbrush. I applied this post shade with my Iwata Custom Micron airbrush, concentrating around detail, and areas that would get worn and dirty. This is also a great time to apply rain and dirt streaks. This technique adds a general griminess to the model, making it looked lived in and worn. At this stage I also painted the smaller details in like road wheel tyres and axe handles.

I wanted to include a tarpaulin on the vehicle, something the crew have rigged up to protect themselves from the elements. I feel the best product to use for this is a two-part epoxy putty called Epoxie Sculpt. After thoroughly mixing the two parts, I rolled the blob of putty into a very thin sheet, using

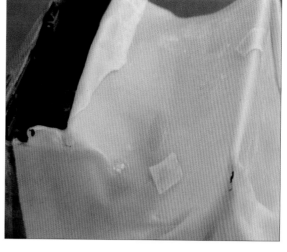

Vehicle foul weather tarp made from thinly rolled Epoxie Sculpt. This putty is very easy to work with. The small retaining straps were also made from Epoxie Sculpt.

For increased realism, I added tiny patches in the tarp.

talcum powder to stop it sticking to my cutting mat. I carefully draped this thin layer of putty over the kit's tarp tilts, making sure the tarp was draped and hung realistically. Once the putty was partially cured, I trimmed it to size, and left it to cure fully. I also added small patches from Epoxie Sculpt, just to add a little interest. A final touch for the tarp was to add small retaining straps, also from Epoxie Sculpt.

Weathering

While the tarp was curing, I set about applying the mud to the running gear. This is the bit I really enjoy. I make my mud from artists' acrylic texture gel mixed with various brown pastel chalk, and lots of static grass. This adds some great texture to what would otherwise be smooth texture-less mud. I applied the mud with a small flat brush, making sure I got it into all the nooks and crannies within the running gear. This mix was also applied to the tracks, though they were not overwhelmed. As this mud was drying, I sprinkled a mix of brown and sand coloured pastels over the wheels, just to add to the look of randomly coloured mud and gunk.

The fighting compartment interior was weathered with pastel chalks, in shades of dark brown. I added 1/35-scale muddy footprints by using Calibre 35's boot prints. These are literally tiny resin boots that, when dipped into pastels or mud mix and walked over the model, leave very convincing foot-prints. I like to add a metal sheen to my models and added chips and scrapes with a 2B clutch pencil, applying larger areas of wear by rubbing the model with my finger dipped in 2B pencil shavings. Not very scientific I know, but it adds a subtle sheen to everything.

By now the tarp was dry and can be popped off the model for painting. After a quick coat of light grey green, I applied various brown and sand coloured pastels quite heavily. Over this I brushed clean Tamiya enamel thinners. This acts to blend in the pastels, and bind them to the surface of the tarp. When the thinners has dried, the pastels can be softened by stippling them with a stiff bush and, as a final touch, I applied rain marks on the tarp by lightly streaking a slightly wet brush in a downward motion over the sides and back of the tarp. The tarp can then be glued permanently to the model. Once attached, I added two tie-down wires to the rear of the tarp, an antenna to the rubber antenna boot, and the model was complete.

Applying the mud mix.

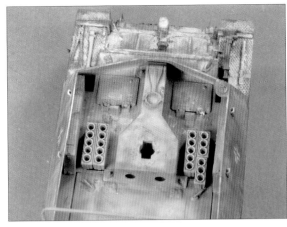

Weathering the interior. I made sure there were lots of muddy and dirty boot prints as well as paint scratches.

Adding wear to the gun. A 2B pencil is best for simulating metal wear and sheen.

After applying pastel chalks to the tarp, seal it in by brushing clean Tamiya thinners on. Once dry, the pastel adheres to the tarp nicely.

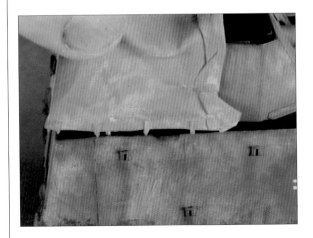

Glue the tarp to the kit. Note the pastels have yet to be blended to sit naturally on the tarp.

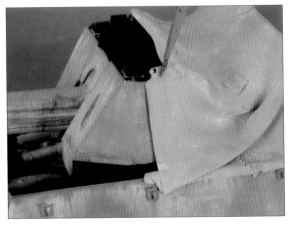

Add rain streaks with a wet brush. I just wet the brush with water, then streak in a downward motion.

ABOVE, BELOW AND NEXT PAGE Views of the finished model.

Marder III mit PaK36r

Subject:	Panzerjäger 38(t) für 7.62cm PaK36r 'Marder III'
Skill Level:	Advanced
Base Kit:	Tamiya Marder III MM35248
Scale:	1/35
Additional detailing sets used:	Aber detail set (35100)
	Aber fenders (35101)
	K59 resin gun and shield
	K59 replacement upper armour
	CMK interior for Marder III (3022)
	Friulmodel ATL 53 38t/Marder tracks

History

This Marder III was based on Panzerkampfwagen 38(t) light tank. It was designated Panzerjäger 38(t) für 7.62cm PaK36(r), and, like the Marder II Ausf. D, was armed with a captured Soviet 76.2mm PaK 36(r) L/51 anti-tank gun. The standard 38(t) light tank, with its turret and superstructure removed, was fitted with a cruciform gun mount and 10–50mm-thick armour to form a fighting compartment for a four-man crew. The fighting compartment was open at the top and rear, with the gun shield being virtually identical to the Marder II Ausf. D. The vehicle carried 30 rounds of ammunition in vertical and horizontal racks beneath the gun. A 7.92mm MG37(t) Besa machine gun was mounted in the front hull.

Three hundred and forty-four Marder IIIs were produced by BMM in Prague from April to November 1942, with an additional 19 converted in 1943. Marder IIIs were issued to Panzerjäger Abteilungen and served mainly on the Eastern Front; 66 were also delivered to North Africa in 1942. There are photographs of Marder IIIs being used in France as late as 1944.

The model

Tamiya's beautiful model of the Marder III was released in 2001. The kit incorporates an incredible level of accuracy, fine rivet detail on the upper armour, delicate detail around the gun, and very accurate running gear. Built out of the box, it can be made into a fantastic model.

As with any kit though, there is always room for improvement. There are an abundance of aftermarket detail sets available for the Marder III now that it's been available for a few years. As you can see down into the driver's and radio operator's compartment on the Marder III, I wanted to include the interior to this section. The first step is to prepare the Tamiya kit parts, ready to accept the CMK interior. As a by-product of the injection moulding process, the interior surfaces of the kit were marred with round knock-out pin marks. These were filled with Tamiya grey putty and, once dry, sanded smooth.

Construction

With a project like this, it's important to think ahead to the painting stage. I wanted to depict this vehicle in North Africa, knocked out and abandoned. This needs to be taken into consideration when building and painting the kit. Also, there are some areas that, once the main kit is assembled, won't be accessible enough to paint. Based on this, I chose to build, paint, and weather the interior before moving onto the outside of the kit. CMK have in their ever-expanding

Sd.Kfz.139 7.62cm Pak36 r auf Gw.38

1 35 ミリタリーミニチュアシリーズ NC

ドイツ対戦車自走砲マーダー

(7.62cm Pak36搭)

★ 主砲装備など戦闘室も精密
★ 緊迫感あふれる車員の人形2

GERMAN TANK DESTROYER

MARDER III

1/35 MILITARY MINIATURE SERIES No.248
★ HIGHLY ACCURATE STATIC DISPLAY MODEL ★ COMPLETE EXTERIOR
AND LOADING BREECH DETAILING ★ MOVABLE GUN WITH GUNSIGHT
★ SEATS AND GUN FIXING CLAMP CAN BE ASSEMBLED IN TWO POSITIONS
★ INCLUDES TWO CREW FIGURES

★ READY TO ASSEMBLE PRECISION MODEL KIT
★ MODELING SKILLS HELPFUL IF UNDER 10 YEARS OF AGE
★ CEMENT AND PAINT NOT INCLUDED

TAMIYA

Tamiya Marder III box art.

inventory both driver's interior and engine bay detail sets. On this kit I only used the interior set. These sets consist of resin and photo-etched brass, and are extremely detailed. I started by adding detail from the CMK set to the side interior walls. As I intended to model a derelict vehicle, I omitted some parts from the interior, and modelled some bent and damaged. For example, I left out the driver's seat altogether, and added some bent riveted flange detail above the driver's position from Evergreen plastic strip.

First step in painting the interior is to apply what's known as a pre-shade. This is, as the name suggests, a dark spray coat, sprayed around all detail. It doesn't

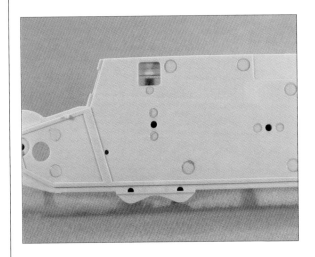

Internal hull wall. Knock-out pins circled for attention.

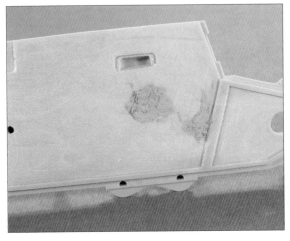

Knock-out pins filled and sanded.

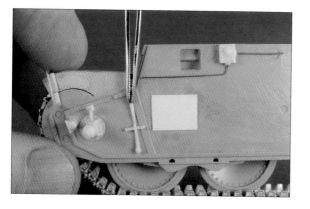

ABOVE AND ABOVE RIGHT Adding the CMK Marder III interior. This set is designed well and fits perfectly.

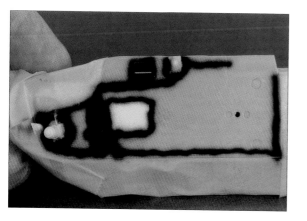

First step when painting – apply the pre-shade with Tamiya XF1 Matt Black. Concentrate around details.

Next, spray on the interior colour mix. See how the pre-shade is just visible.

matter if the painted lines are straight, or if there is paint spatter, as this is only the first of many coats of paint. I applied Tamiya XF1 Matt Black as a pre-shade coat. Once this was touch dry, I sprayed a mix of Gunze H318 Radome and H11 Flat White. German interiors were painted an off-white colour known as *elfenbein*. I sprayed a coat just dark enough to cover the sand-coloured plastic, but translucent enough that the pre-shade was still visible. The next step is to paint in any detail that's not meant to be *elfenbein* – intercom boxes, transmission, steering gear, and seats. These components were painted now, as they would wear and get weathered at the same rate as the main interior paint colour. It's easier to do this in one step, rather than weathering each component individually. Next I applied a post shade. This really dirties up the paint nicely. I made sure that I applied it in a streaky pattern, helping to simulate rain marks (remember, it's an open-topped vehicle!). I applied lots of brown pastel chalk dust to the interior floor, and finalised the weathering process by applying lots of paint chips and wear with a 2B pencil. The transmission was weathered with a thick oily wash of turpentine and artist oil paint, and then a metallic sheen was added with a 2B pencil. The radios were left out of the interior, supposedly scavenged by maintenance crew to stop them falling into the hands of the Allies.

Before I set the lower hull aside, I built up both the running gear, and Aber's excellent photo-etched (PE) brass fenders. Many people shy away from using etched brass, but it's an excellent medium for modelling. It's easy to work with (with the right tools!) and holds excellent detail. I used Cyanoacrylate to bind

Now the post shade has been applied. The post shade really makes the paint look worn and tired.

Pastels applied heavily to the hull floor and sides. Paint chips added, as well as substantial paint wear. I also added some leftover radio cabling from fine solder.

The basic Aber photo-etched fender.

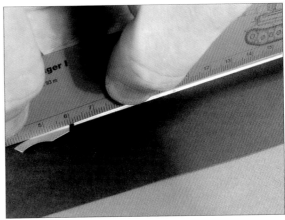

I used a sturdy metal ruler to bend the entire fender in one go. Use a hard surface to push the fender against when bending.

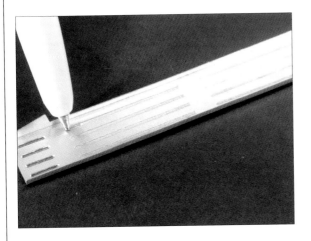

Once bent, the strengthening ribs can be added using a ballpoint pen.

Carefully trim the Tamiya parts with a razor saw. Watch out, razor saws are sharp!

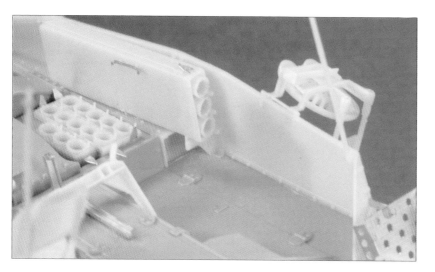

K59 hull armour added to the Tamiya fighting compartment floor. The ammunition bins and crew seats are also added now.

Front plate detail. Note the 2-pdr solid shot AP round hit above the driver's visor. German armour plate was quite brittle and would often crack when hit. Resin is perfect for simulating this, it snaps rather than bends.

Fenders without stowage. This vehicle is abandoned, so no tool stowage was fitted.

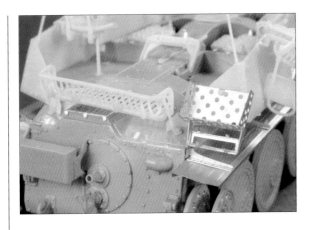

Hull rear. The fine resin basket is a K59 part, the etched-brass basket is an Aber item.

Fighting compartment interior. No stowage added here either, all the ammo racks are left empty.

the etch to the resin and plastic. It also pays to use the best – Aber. Aber make two detail sets for the Marder III, a set that covers detail all over the vehicle, and a fender set. Start by removing the fenders from the sprue. At this stage they are flat and virtually featureless. I tend to shy away from dedicated photo-etch benders; I prefer to bend brass using tools already on hand – metal rulers, pliers, and tweezers. Take the fender, line up the pre-etched bend line with the edge of a sturdy metal ruler, and push against a hard surface, I usually use a small piece of safety glass or a porcelain tile. By using a ruler, and working slowly, the whole bent-over lip on the fender can be bent at once. Damage can be incorporated at this stage, but keep one thing in mind. It's best to build the fender perfectly first, then add the damage in later. If the fender is bent poorly, then damage added its forever going to look like a shoddy job was done in the first place. Once both lips have been bent over, the ribs can be added by running a fine ball point pen in the half-etched grooves. This entire process probably takes as long as it took you to read this paragraph thus far. This bending technique, while used to describe the construction of the fenders, extends itself to all the etch brass used on the entire vehicle.

Moving to the upper hull, we get to incorporate another detail set – well two actually. K59 is a small company out of Hong Kong with a huge reputation. The quality of their resin casting is astounding. Virtually the entire upper superstructure, including the gun and gun shield, can be replaced with the K59 resin sets. Of course there is nothing wrong with the Tamiya part, that is until you see the K59 bits! The Tamiya upper hull was carefully trimmed with a fine razor saw, making way for the replacement resin parts. The resin K59 parts can be added mostly as per instructions, with a couple of exceptions. I wanted to show a hit on the front armour plate, so I drilled an appropriately sized hole in the part, scribed some crack lines, and literally snapped the part. The beauty of resin is that it's quite brittle, so snaps when bent, just like a lot of German World War II armour plate.

The fenders were detailed using the remainder of the Aber detail set, and the beautiful K59 fire extinguisher. I wanted to show all of the tools missing, and their associated clamps empty, so the Aber clamps were laboriously constructed without glue, then carefully glued to the fenders. The delicate K59 rear stowage basket can be added at this stage, as can all the fighting compartment stowage, seats, ammo racks, and MP38/40 rack. Of course the ammo and gun racks were left empty, and one of the crew seats arranged in a haphazard manner, indicating the crew left in a hurry. The last part of construction concerns the gun and upper armour, replacing the kit gun with the turned aluminium and resin replacement parts in the K59 set.

Marder III primed. Tamiya grey primer was used to get a uniform surface to apply the camouflage coat.

First camouflage coat – Vallejo Air German Grey.

Painting

The first step when painting this Marder, or any kit where multiple media are used, is to prime all the parts. This gives a uniform base for the ensuing camouflage coats. I used Tamiya light grey surface primer. For paint on this Marder, I used Vallejo Model Air acrylic paint for airbrushes. The tank was given an overall coat of 052 German Grey, and left to dry. I left the paint to full harden overnight, and then applied Winsor & Newton artist masking fluid randomly with a piece of green kitchen scourer. This artist masking fluid is a latex rubber solution, and is applied with the scourer to randomly cover sections of German Grey paint. This mask only takes a couple of minutes to dry, then I applied a sparse coat of Model Color 976 Buff. I wanted this coat to patchily cover the grey, and to look hastily applied. I left the inside of the gun shield area in grey.

Now once the sand paint was dry, I set about removing the latex with a toothbrush, and a stiff bristled paintbrush. The latex just peels off, leaving a fantastically chipped effect. The next step was applying a post shade. I concentrated on applying stains where the crew worked when fighting, and where they'd hold on while traversing rough ground, i.e. handles and edges of the armour plate.

Next I thought I'd try a technique I've seen many modellers do, but never actually tried myself. It involves applying streaks of different coloured oil paints, then blending these streaks in with a large brush and clean white spirit thinners.

Applying the latex mask with a green kitchen scourer. The scourer allows the rubber to be applied in a random fashion.

39

Once the rubber has been removed, the model looks like the sand coloured camouflage paint has worn and chipped off in the harsh desert environment.

This is to simulate rain and dirt streaks. Simply apply the streaks in a random fashion with a fine brush, and then blend them in with a wide brush moistened with white spirit. As you can see, it imparts a realistic streaky and worn appearance.

Weathering

Remembering this vehicle is depicted in North Africa, abandoned and shot up, I wanted to make the weathering heavy. We have started this by having the basic paint scheme dramatically chipped. I continued on this theme by applying a heavy coat of pastel chalk to the lower hull and running gear. I literally applied this with a wide brush, and then secured it to the model by brushing clean water over it. Once the water dries, the pastel chalk stains the hull and wheels nicely, and doesn't crumble off. This effect was continued to a certain extent on the upper hull and gun shield, but in these areas pastels were applied in a more patchy manner.

Rather than use the kit supplied tracks, which are nice, I chose to use Friulmodellisimo white metal individual tracks. The tracks were built, painted,

Random streaks of artist's oil paints. This paint shouldn't be allowed to dry.

The streaks after being blended with clean thinners. This process is subtle, but really adds a nice faded appearance to the model.

and weathered as per the Marder I in the first chapter. I fitted the tracks after I had partially weathered the lower hull, Friul tracks are heavy, and I didn't want to damage anything by handling them to much. Applying Rustall, an alcohol-based solution that literally rusts anything, rusted the tracks. Once the Rustall had dried, I enhanced the rusty finish on the track with an orange pencil. If not in use, the metal in tank tracks rusts to bright orange virtually overnight.

Now that the kit was nearing completion, there were a couple more areas to attend to. As touched on previously, I like to add a metal shine to my tanks. This imparts an additional lived-in look. Once again, I applied the metal sheen by rubbing the model with a finger that had been dipped in 2B pencil shavings. This effect was concentrated around areas of high wear, the gun and its controls, and the fighting compartment floor. The edges of the hull armour plate also received some attention. One final touch was to add blown hub seals to all the road wheels. Pick any photograph of knocked-out or abandoned World War II vehicles, and there is evidence of the wheel bearings having 'let go' and leaked bearing grease onto the road wheel. This final weathering effect was added by applying a thick oil paint and white spirit wash to each road wheel centre.

An antenna was attached, and bent, and the model was complete.

Large amounts of pastels added to the wheels and running gear.

Blend these pastels with clean Tamiya thinners, or water. When dry, the pastels look like dried mud and dust. Contrary to popular belief, there was mud and water in the desert!

Fitting the Friul track. I made sure the join in the track was at the sprocket just for added strength. Slide the last track pin wire in and snip off the excess with side cutters.

As this vehicle has been left for some time, make the tracks look a little rusty. I used Rustall to make the tracks appear covered in rust.

An orange pencil is also good for adding a rusty appearance to the tracks. Note the rusty ring around each road wheel. In normal travel, this section of wheel comes in contact with the track, and is polished bright silver. Left for a while, this too rusts.

Add wear to the fighting compartment floor by rubbing a finger dipped in lead pencil shavings. This adds a lot of metal sheen to this area.

When a vehicle stands for any length of time, the hub seals in the centre of road wheels seems to leak oil and grease. This is a very common feature, and was added to the model with a heavy oil paint wash.

ABOVE, BELOW AND NEXT PAGE **Views** of the finished model.

Marder III Ausf. M

Subject:	Panzerjäger 38(t) mit 7.5cm PaK40/3 Ausf. M 'Marder III Ausf. M'
Skill Level:	Advanced
Base Kit:	Tamiya Marder III Ausf. M (35225)
Scale:	1/35
Additional detailing sets used:	TMD Marder III Ausf. M early backdate Aber fenders (35126) Aber detail set (35125) ModelKasten workable track (SK30)

History

The Marder III Ausf. M was also based on the Panzerkampfwagen 38(t) Ausf. M chassis. Its designation was Panzerjäger 38(t) mit 7.5cm PaK40/3 Ausf. M. Like the Marder III Ausf. H, it was armed with the 75mm PaK 40/3 L/46 anti-tank gun and operated by a crew of four. The fighting compartment was quite unlike any other vehicle in the Marder family, with a large overhang past the rear idler wheels, and the gun and upper armour mounted at the middle and rear of the vehicle respectively. Typical of Marders, the fighting compartment of Ausf. M was open only at the top. Consensus is that the vehicle carried 27 rounds of PaK 40 ammunition, but the vehicle on display at Saumur Musée des Blindés in France has ammunition racks under the floor plates in the fighting compartment.

The model

There isn't much to say in relation to the quality of this Marder III Ausf. M by Tamiya. It's truly an amazing kit, loads of detail both inside and outside the vehicle. Without trying to sound like a broken record when it comes to Tamiya kits, they can be built out of box to form a great model, or detailed to get yourself a masterpiece. I of course chose to detail the hell out of it. The Tamiya kit represents a late model Ausf. M, with a square welded driver's hood and external exhaust pipe. These are the two main features that differentiate an early from a late variant.

Construction

In previous chapters, we have discussed working with resin and with etched brass, and in this chapter, I wanted to incorporate a new technique – soldering. Soldering is a method of joining metal parts together in a solid permanent bond. The main advantage of soldering is the strength of the join. A disadvantage is that it's a little time consuming, using a hot iron can also be dangerous.

I find the best way to approach soldering is to build or bend the brass parts as if they were to be joined with CA glue. Once the parts are bent to shape, assess where the solder is to go on the parts. We'll use the Aber etched-brass fenders as an example. I indented all the strengthening ribs and bent over the edges as per the instructions, then worked out that it would be best to solder the underside of the front edge of each fender. I plugged the soldering iron in and let it get up to temperature. I use a very cheap one I picked up at an electronics store. While I was there I grabbed some fine solid core solder and thin brushable flux. When the iron is up to temperature, I touched the tip of the iron to some solder, getting a ball of solder on the tip. This was wiped off

Tamiya Marder III Ausf. M box art.

on a damp kitchen sponge, leaving the tip with a smooth silver finish. This is what's known as 'tinning' the soldering iron. Next, brush some flux into the join on the etched fender. The flux I use has the consistency of water. Now, touch the iron to the area to be joined, and once the brass gets hot enough, the solder will flow from the iron into the join – perfectly. The solder will only flow where the flux is, which makes it important to ensure you are careful only to flux the area to be joined. The solder takes only a second to harden, and then you can clean up any excess with a file or sandpaper. This process was repeated with the support brackets and tool mounts on the upper side of the fenders. This was the first time I'd soldered, and it only took me a few minutes to master the technique.

The lower hull was built up as per the Tamiya kit instructions, but at an early stage I decided that I wanted to depict a particular vehicle. The vehicle was a Marder III Ausf. M in Italy, captured by elements of the 8th Indian Infantry Division. The Marder was originally on the roster of Pz.Jg.Abt.165,

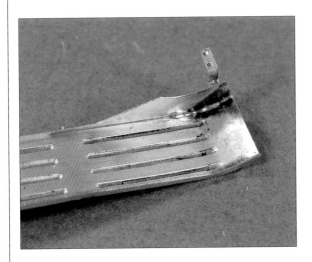

Underside of soldered fender. Note how the solder has run along the inner corners. With the iron at he right temperature, and with the right amount of the flux, the solder just flows along the join.

Any excess solder can be removed with a file or some wet and dry sandpaper.

Grouser box. This entire assembly was soldered together.

ModelKasten 38t tracks. Marders tended to carry a lot of spare track.

The grey resin is the Tiger Model Designs Marder III Ausf. M backdate kit. The upper hull fits well to the Tamiya kit as can be seen here.

Aber tool clamps and engine hatch handles can be added, as can the rest of the Tamiya kit parts.

Hull rear. The realistic sit of the tow cable was achieved by brushing the nylon string with Mr Surfacer.

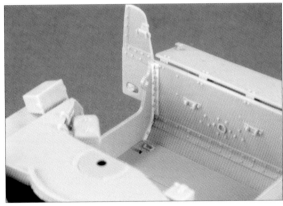

Fighting compartment interior. Early Marder III Ausf. M's had a lot of extra ribbing and rivets when compared to later versions. This ribbing was added from Evergreen styrene strip, and rivets left over from the Marder II earlier in the book.

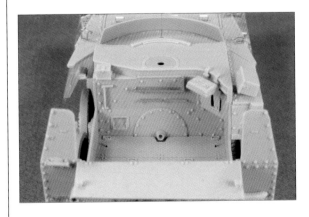

Another Marder, another abandoned vehicle! The crew stowage was left out of the interior, I used Aber's empty MP40 rack and ammo pouch clips here.

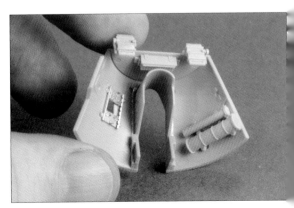

Interior of the curved gun shield. This area can be detailed with both TMD and Aber parts.

part of the German 65th Infantry Division. This vehicle is depicted on pages 48 and 49 of the excellent Nuts & Bolts 17 on the Marder III Ausf. M. The vehicle has been repainted, but the barrel and fighting compartment interior remain in the original German camouflage. Allied markings have been painted on the sides and rear of the vehicle in a distinctive and interesting way – the minute I saw it I just knew I had to model this vehicle.

Tiger Model Designs (TMD) has just released a Marder III Ausf. M backdate conversion for the Tamiya kit. This resin set replaces just about the entire upper portion of the kit with the correct parts for an early version. I started backdating the Tamiya kit by adding the upper hull roof. This section contains the rounded cast driver's hood. Onto this, I added spare track links from ModelKasten. The previously soldered fenders were attached at this time as well. I wanted to depict all the vehicle stowage missing, and their brackets empty. I added the etched Aber brackets to the hull top at the same time.

The hull rear plate was replaced with the corresponding item from the TMD set, trimmed to fit. The TMD set contained a replacement crew ladder, but I used the Aber replacement, as it is a truer representation of how it looked. I added two vehicle tow ropes using Tamiya Panzer IV tow-rope eyes, and some twine. This was coated in Mr Surfacer 1000 to stiffen it up. The internal face of the rear plate was detailed with strip and rivets scavenged from the Tamiya parts that were not used as a result of backdating the kit.

Moving onto the interior of the fighting compartment, I built the TMD resin parts up as per instructions, adding only the main gun ammunition, as per photographs of the real vehicle. It would seem that everything else, i.e. radios, crew gear, personal weapons, and stowage, was removed by either the crew when they abandoned the vehicle, or by the new owners. All the empty brackets for these items were added using the Aber etch detail set. The gun and inner gun shield were detailed as well using the TMD and Aber sets.

Painting

As with the Marders in the previous chapters, it was necessary to paint the fighting compartment and gun before gluing the upper hull together. This area looks to have remained in its original German-applied livery, so I airbrushed a coat of Humbrol 93 Desert Sand. Mixed with its own thinners, Humbrol paint sprays well, leaving a nice matt finish to weather. Again, the interior parts were post shaded to impart a grimy appearance. With this Marder, I also applied a 'filter', or what is more commonly known as a wash. This has been discussed in earlier chapters, and was concentrated around detail and on the floor plates.

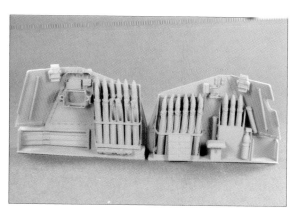

Fighting compartment interior walls. Compare these to the Marder I. The Marder III Ausf. M has a lot of interior stowage. I left the radios out, as this vehicle was captured by the British.

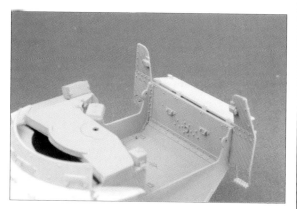

With a coat of paint on, its impossible to tell what's a kit part, what's a TMD resin part, and what's scratch-built.

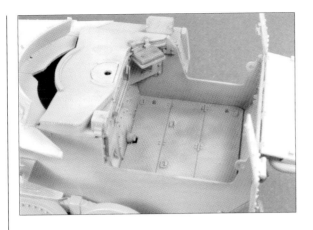

Once the weathering process begins, the hull interior takes on a more realistic look. To my eye, an unweathered model looks toy like and lifeless.

Adding pastels to the interior. I try to weather all the interior components at the same time, for consistency of finish.

Interior finished. Paint chips can be added using Vallejo paint, a 2B lead pencil and a Derwent Black pencil. All combine to create a very worn appearance.

Finished model ready for paint. Temporarily fit the tracks now to adjust for fit.

Once all the details had been painted in with Humbrol enamels, I could continue the weathering process by depicting chipped paint with a 2B and brown pencil and lots of dusty sand/brown-coloured pastels. The Italian theatre seemed to be either extremely hot, dry, and dusty, or cold, wet, and muddy. Images of the vehicle I was modelling seemed to suggest it was dusty and dry, so I weathered the interior accordingly. Once the fighting compartment was weathered, I could permanently affix the side armour, and move onto painting the distinctive camouflage pattern. The ModelKasten tracks were fitted at this stage to see that they lined up correctly.

When I was painting the interior, I applied the same base coat to the entire gun and gun tube. Pictures indicated that these parts remained in the original camouflage after capture and repaint. Accordingly, the gun and interior was masked off and a coat of Tamiya grey primer was sprayed on the model. The colour plate of this vehicle in Nuts & Bolts 17 shows the vehicle in a hand-painted mid-stone and olive green camouflage pattern. So I painted the first colour, Humbrol 73 Matt Bronze Green with the airbrush. I began to weather this coat by mixing up a lighter tone of the same colour, and spraying the centre of all panels, and some downward streaks in the vertical hull plates.

With the gun and interior masked off, apply a primer coat. Use Tamiya grey primer.

First camouflage coat applied. Mixed correctly, Humbrol paint does airbrush well. The road wheels will be painted at a later stage.

Now we can start fading the first camo colour. A light green mix was airbrushed in a random streaky pattern.

Blu-Tack is used to mask off the areas to remain green. This is a cheap, inexpensive and effective way to mask. The Blu-Tack can be reused, and doesn't harm the paint surface.

Once the mid stone colour has dried, I used a white pencil to rough out where the hand-applied markings were to go.

ABOVE **Now the running gear can be painted. I used Humbrol enamels to paint this area. The roundel on the hull side was hand painted with Tamiya acrylics.**

RIGHT **The exhaust and tow cables can be painted with the post shade mix in the airbrush.**

I used Blu-Tack to mask the areas that were to remain in olive green. This putty is usually used to hang posters, and is great for masking as it leaves no residue. Once I had the blobs of Blu-Tack positioned correctly, I airbrushed on a coat of Humbrol 187 Sand. The Blu-Tack easily peels off to reveal a perfectly masked hard-edge camouflage. scheme. Another option would have been to hand paint this pattern – I'm no good at that, I've always preferred using the airbrush. The markings on this vehicle would need to be hand painted, so I used a white pencil to mark out where the roundels on each hull side were to be positioned. I used the pics of the real vehicle as my guide. The roundels and 8th Indian Inf. Div. arm of service markings, along with the 'Z' marking of the previous German owners, were all hand painted with Tamiya acrylic paint. Once the markings were on, I blended all the divergent colours in with a light post shade. I also used the post shade to paint the tow cables and the exhaust pipe.

Weathering

As in the previous chapter, I applied some streaking to the vertical surfaces by daubing on streaks of oil paint, and blending these in with a wide brush moistened with white spirit. The ModelKasten tracks were painted with a very

Streaks of Winsor & Newton oil paint added to replicate rain streaks.

When blended, these streaks give a subtle faded effect.

Weathering the ModelKasten tracks. This photo was taken shortly before the entire run of track fell apart. Note to self, don't use white spirit to make mud mix!

Weathering the hull armour. I added tiny paint chips and scratches with an orange pencil.

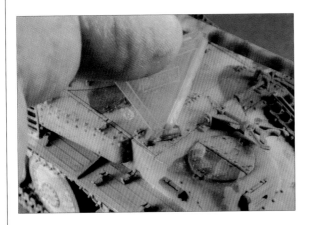

Adding boot prints using the Calibre 35 resin boots. Just dunk the boots into any dusty coloured pastel, and literally walk it over the model, concentrating in areas of high crew traffic.

Add final paint chips of the original German camouflage wearing through the new British camouflage.

dark brown mixed from Tamiya XF64 Red Brown and XF1 Matt Black. I then made up a slurry of earth tone pastel chalks and white spirit, and liberally applied it to the tracks and running gear. Unfortunately, the white spirit ate away the delicate plastic trackpins, and most of the track actually fell apart. Well, I made it four chapters into the book before I was beset by disaster. I laboriously glued the links back together, setting them on the model to get the sag just right.

To finish off the weathering process, and the model, there are a couple of extra areas to attend to. Firstly, I wanted to add some scratches in the paintwork on the sides of the vehicle. I simply used the back end of a paintbrush, and scraped it along the side of the model. I also added some tiny rust-coloured chips using an orange pencil. Also, I wanted to add dusty and dirty boot prints to the areas where the crew would walk on the real vehicle. I added them to the fenders, fighting compartment floor, and hull top/engine deck. A final touch is to add some paint chips of the original German camouflage colour – dark yellow. I added these chips sparingly along the top edges of the hull armour, and around the drivers hatch. These chips, in conjunction with chips added using a 2B pencil, add to the lived in grungy look and finish the vehicle nicely.

ABOVE, BELOW AND NEXT PAGE Views of the finished model.

56

Special feature – 'Yesterday's Hero'

Diorama 'Yesterday's Hero'	
Skill Level:	*Special feature*
Base Kit:	*Italeri Marder III Ausf. H*
Scale:	*1/35*
Additional detailing sets used:	*Royal Model Marder III Ausf. H details (298)*
	Royal Model Marder III Ausf. H Interior (299)
	Gun from Tamiya Marder III Ausf. M
	Wheels from Tamiya Marder III Ausf. M
	Moskit Marder III Ausf. H exhaust (3532)

History

The development of the Marder III Ausf. H was closely linked to that of the Ausf. M. The Marder III Ausf. H was based on the Panzer 38(t) Ausf. H, which in itself was developed purely as a base for self-propelled guns. This chassis was never used to build a conventional tank. As such, the Marder III Ausf. H shared many similarities with the Ausf. M – both mounted the 7.5cm PaK 40/2 gun, both had a crew of four. Having said that, the design of the two was quite different, the H had the engine mounted at the rear, and the M had a mid-mounted engine. Both drove their tracks with a front-mounted sprocket. The H carried 11 more rounds of ammunition in racks mounted within the hull and upper superstructure. Four hundred and seventeen Marder III Ausf. Hs were produced from November 1942, both new vehicles and ones converted from old gun tanks. The Ausf. H mainly served in Russia and on the Eastern Front, but also in Italy. It is also believed to have served in Tunisia.

The model

The Italian model company Italeri first released their Marder III Ausf. H in 1972. For its time, it was an excellent kit, with fine detail and working suspension. Over the years the kit has been withdrawn from the catalogue and reissued numerous times. The H was a bit of a compromise, with many parts shared with Italeri's 38t and Hetzer kits. The kit is looking a bit tired now, especially compared to recent releases. It still remains one of Italeri's better kits, which doesn't say much for Italeri. I used three detail sets from Royal Model, also from Italy. These sets are incredibly comprehensive, replacing the upper armour, fenders, interior, and exterior stowage.

Construction

I started by soldering all the fender parts together. I used the same technique as mentioned in the previous chapter. To clean up any errant solder, I used a wire brush in a small electric motor tool. The solder joins are so strong that they weren't damaged at all by this cleaning process. I attached the fenders at this stage along with the running gear. Italeri's running gear is pretty woeful; I ordered individual wheel sprues from the Tamiya Marder III Ausf. M, direct from Rainbow 10 in Japan. The Tamiya wheels didn't need much coaxing to fit onto the Italeri suspension arms.

The Royal Model set includes a full hull interior for the Marder III Ausf. H; its inclusion is a real necessity in such an open-topped vehicle. I built up the resin interior components separate from the hull as I wanted these items removable

MARDER III AUSF. H

ITALERI

1:35
MODEL KIT / M
No

Italeri Marder III Ausf. H box art.

for painting. I lined the internal walls and floor with .005in. Evergreen plastic card for a uniform surface. Internal hull components included in the Royal Model sets were attached now. I also added an ammunition rack to the front right side hull interior. Pictures in Nuts & Bolts 18 on the Marder III Ausf. H indicate a rack was situated here. I used a rack left over from the Marder III Ausf. M in the last chapter.

I painted the interior with Xtracolour X818 German Interior Cream. This is enamel paint, and I think it's a pretty good match to surviving examples of *elfenbein* paint. The transmission was painted Tamiya XF22 RLM Grey.

As per usual, I applied a post shade as the first step in the weathering process. I concentrated this effect into the corners and the floor area. Being enamel, Xtracolour paint doesn't respond well to a traditional thinner-based wash or filter. I applied pastel chalks quite heavily to the floor and sides of the hull interior, and then brushed on clean water. Once the water dries, it leaves the pastels adhered to the hull areas in a fairly random pattern, i.e. it doesn't look painted on!

Continuing with the weathering process, I applied paint chips to the engine firewall, drive shaft cover and the transmission itself with a 2B pencil. I made sure those areas of high wear received the most attention with the pencil, edges of the transmission, access hatches on the firewall, the floor. I added turned-brass ammunition to the internal rack. This ammo is from Tamiya, and is actually not a full round, but just enough to fit in the ammo racks. The projectiles were painted semi-gloss black, and only weathered lightly with pastel chalks.

From working on the interior, I moved to the construction outside of the vehicle. The Marder III Ausf. H had a quite distinctive basket arrangement on the rear of the hull. The Italeri parts are quite usable; I chose to thin them down rather than replace them. I used a Flexi file to laboriously thin down each section of the rearmost basket. It actually sounds more daunting and tedious than it is to do – I just worked in sections, making sure I didn't miss any areas.

Soldered front fender.

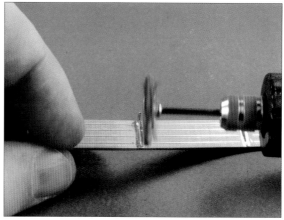

Cleaning excess solder with a wire brush in a motor tool. This is an effective way of cleaning errant solder. The join is so strong, it won't be damaged by the wire brush.

Fenders fitted to the Italeri Hull. I've also applied the Tamiya wheels, which, surprisingly, were a perfect fit to the Italeri hull.

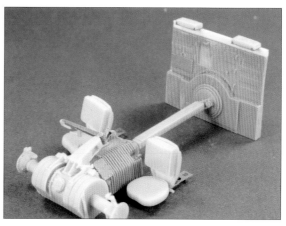

Royal Model interior parts.

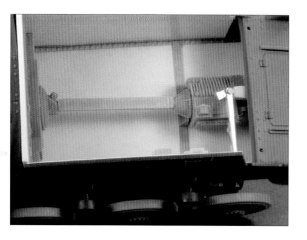

I lined the hull interior with .005in. Evergreen plastic card. This provided a uniform surface for detailing.

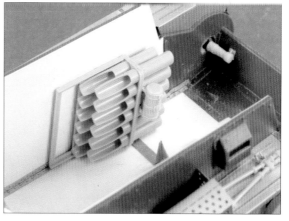

Ammunition rack added to the hull interior. This is a Tamiya part left over from the Marder III Ausf. M.

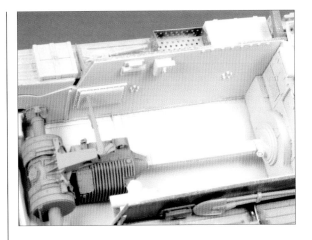

Basic paint colours applied to the hull interior.

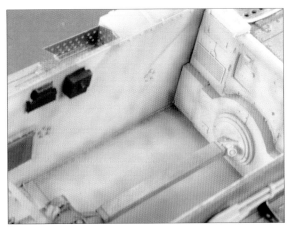

The hull interior after a post shade. Compared to the previous picture, it's starting to look dirty and lived in.

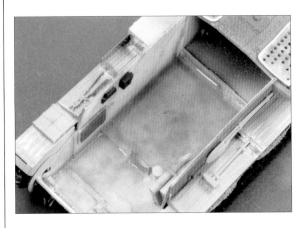

Water applied to the dry pastels on the hull floor; you can speed up the drying process by using a hair dryer.

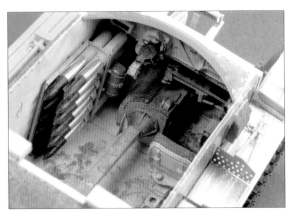

ABOVE AND BELOW LEFT Fully weathered hull interior. The brass of the Tamiya turned ammunition really stands out against the drab interior.

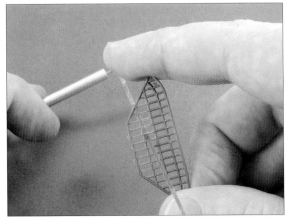

Carefully thinning down the rear stowage basket. Gingerly using a Flexi file here will result in a much finer basket. Compare the area already thinned down to the area not yet done.

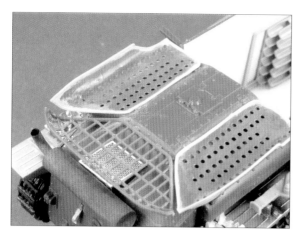

Side stowage baskets. Thin these down as well, and replace the tubular edging with Evergreen styrene rod.

Hull rear. The Moskit metal exhaust is a great addition, but very fragile.

Fender stowage added from Tamiya and Royal Model parts.

Tamiya Marder III tracks added. I avoided using expensive aftermarket tracks as the vehicle would be attached to a diorama base.

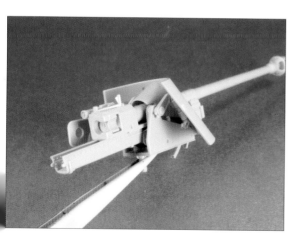

Replace the Italeri gun with a Tamiya PaK 40 from the Marder III M. The III Ausf. H and M utilized the same gun.

Upper armour interior. The Royal Model armour was carefully bent to shape, soldered together, then the interior was detailed as per photographs from the Nuts & Bolts book.

Radio installation. This entire part was from the Royal Model kit, and is mostly etched brass. The periscope and radio junction box are resin items.

Royal Model upper armour complete and ready for paint. Note the hundreds of tiny plastic rivets, each added individually.

I heavily thinned the two side perforated baskets with the motor tool and sandpaper. In reality these baskets are thin metal, and really required a lot of thinning. I remade the tubular edges with carefully bent .020in. Evergreen styrene rod. While working on this area, I replaced the kit muffler with the exquisite Moskit metal exhaust. It beats me how they get their mufflers so delicate, but they really are the finest things on the market. It's incredibly fragile, and was carefully glued in place.

The fender stowage was added from a mix of Tamiya Panzer IV OVM and Royal Model resin and etched items. In contrast to other Marders, the fenders on the Marder III Ausf. were fairly uncluttered with stowage. As mentioned earlier, the Tamiya Panzer IV toolset is an absolute must have when detailing any kit (apart from a Tamiya kit of course). I added Royal Model tool brackets to the Tamiya tools, and used leftover Friul tracks from the Marder III in an earlier chapter. I also used the kit tracks from the Tamiya Marder III, these are far better than the Italeri-supplied tracks. As this vehicle is to be permanently attached to a diorama, I didn't want to use expensive ModelKasten or Friul tracks – their detail would be wasted as much of the vehicle is to be dirty and on a base.

The lower hull was set aside, and I started work on the gun and gun shield. While good for its time, the PaK 40 in the Italeri kit needs replacing. The Marder Ausf. III H uses the identical gun to the Marder III Ausf. M. Easy solution – replace the entire gun and frontal curved gun shield with gun parts from the Tamiya Marder III Ausf. M.

The Royal Model sets provide entire upper armour replacement parts in photo-etched nickel-coated brass. I started off by bending the main armour plates to shape, and soldering them for added strength. Each side was assembled separately, and then the roof section was soldered last. An option if you didn't have access to the Royal sets is to trace the kit parts out on .010in. Evergreen styrene sheet, cut out and replace the kit armour. Once assembled, I added the internal braces that come with the Royal sets. I also added the FuG radio installation, entirely out of etched nickel and resin, also included in the Royal Model set. The rest of the upper armour interior was detailed as per pictures in the Nuts & Bolts volume on the Marder III Ausf. H.

Externally, Royal Model suggest in their instructions to add rivets to the armour; these rivets are etched flat, and included in their set. Unfortunately, the rivets used in construction of the Marder are domed-head rivets. I used Grandt Line styrene rivets, 128 of them to be exact. I attached each rivet using CA glue, applied with the tip of a knife blade.

Painting

Finally, I could attend to the painting process. As usual, I commenced by applying a primer coat. This provides something for the ensuing paint to 'bite' into. The model was sprayed with an all over coat of Tamiya acrylic XF59 Desert Yellow. I prefer this colour over XF 60 Dark Yellow, which I feel is too green in shade. Next I applied a broad solid camouflage of Tamiya XF 64 Red Brown and XF62 Olive Drab. Once this had dried, I affixed decals I'd pilfered from the Marder III Ausf. M, well, I should say leftover decals from this Marder. All the small details like roadwheel tyres were painted in, including the tracks which I airbrushed a dark brown mixed from XF64 and XF1 Matt Black. A quick post shade was sprayed on, and then the model was set aside so I could work on the diorama base.

The diorama

I started work on the diorama by first figuring out what I wanted to depict. I liked the idea of a tank crew being photographed by a newsreel photographer, for the German *Wochenschau* (weekly show). I wanted the crew being filmed in

Marder III Ausf. H with a primer coat applied. Covering all the divergent materials in this kit is important to achieve a good paint finish.

Basic camouflage paint scheme applied. I used Tamiya acrylics. The tracks were carefully painted while attached to the model.

Now a post shade can be applied. This begins the weathering process.

front of a knocked-out Russian T-34, in typical propaganda fashion. I began assembling components I wanted to include in the diorama setting. It's not good to discover you've missed some vital ingredient for the scene when you're pouring groundwork! Central to this scene would be the tank crew; I was able to find four excellent, animated figures in the Wolf figure range. I was also able to locate a German combat cameraman from Hornet. MIG Productions make an excellent destroyed T-34, so it was included. The cameraman would need transport, so I chose a Tamiya Schwimmwagen as his ride. As scene fillers, I included some tree stumps as well.

I used Osprey's excellent *Terrain Modelling* book as a guide when constructing the diorama base for this model. This really is a great reference for anyone wanting to build realistic looking diorama groundwork. I worked out the scene layout, and glued some thin polystyrene foam to the base, to slightly elevate the roadway. I used PVA white glue to secure the foam.

I added the groundwork itself from a product called Porion. This is a concrete like material that when dry has a fantastic earth-like texture, if not smoothed over with water. This was applied with a plastic putty trowel, ensuring there was enough material to cover the raised roadway section. Into the wet Porion I pressed the tree stumps, and some matchsticks, to simulate fence posts. I also trimmed some Woodland Scenics 'tall grass' into little bushels, and positioned these around the bases of the fence posts. The diorama groundwork was left to cure; this took a couple of days.

While the base was hardening, I set to work on the figures. I used the sadly out of print Tony Greenland *Panzer Modelling Masterclass* book as a guide to painting the figures. Stefan Müller-Herdemertens' work is featured as a 'how to' in this book, and is incredible. The figures' faces were painted with Winsor & Newton oil paints, over a base coat of Tamiya XF 15 Flat Flesh. A mix of burnt umber, titanium white, and yellow ochre was applied over this, left to 'stain' the Tamiya base coat, and then removed with a broad soft brush. This left a

tiny deposit of paint in the creases on the face, simulating natural shadows. The faces were them highlighted with Titanium white oil paint. A glaze of burnt umber and lamp black was run into the eye sockets, and the ears, to add definition. This same process was repeated for the hands as well. The uniforms were painted with Humbrol enamels, 111 for the grey-green uniforms, and 33 for the black. Details like buttons and piping was picked out with Tamiya acrylics.

Once the base groundwork was dry, I applied the top texture to it using brown tiling grout. I used artists' spray adhesive to secure this. On top of that, I sprayed a very thin dilution of PVA glue mixed with water. As this dries, it cracks the groundwork, imparting a dry, dirty texture. This again was allowed to dry. I made tiny footprints in the fresh soil using Calibre 35's resin boots. Fencing wire was added between the posts using fine fuse wire. The fence posts and tree stumps were weathered by applying an oil paint wash, highlighting the fine detail on them.

The Marder III Ausf. H was now permanently attached to the base. I attached it the same way a bricklayer would attach the next brick to his wall – I applied Porion to the tracks with a trowel, and then pushed the model onto the base, until the Porion 'gooshed' out and the tank sat perfectly flat on the ground. It's

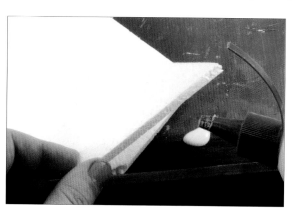

ABOVE AND ABOVE RIGHT **Never throw anything out! This thin polystyrene foam was leftover packaging from a computer. It's perfect for using to change the groundwork level in dioramas.**

Foam is used here so that the level is changed, but the depth of groundwork material stays the same. Porion and brown tile grout make excellent and inexpensive groundwork material.

The basic diorama groundwork applied. Here the Porion is still wet, so all the tree stumps, fence posts and tufts of grass have been pushed into the goo. The vehicles have also been pushed into the base, to mark their position.

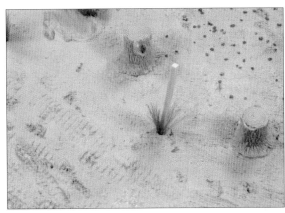

Detail shot of a tree stump, and a fence post. Little details like this add interest to the diorama, which would be boring if it was just a square of groundwork with a tank on it.

Completed figures. Each tank crewmember has assumed a different pose. This is something I wanted when I went looking for appropriate figures, I didn't want four 'robots' just standing there. Note how the standing figures have all shifted their weight over one hip, indicating a relaxed pose.

ABOVE AND BELOW LEFT Close up of the groundwork. To achieve this fresh soil look, I applied simple tiling grout over the Porion. This adds colour. Note the footprints in the soil.

Blending the Marder III H into the groundwork. Here, the vehicle isn't weathered at all. The idea behind this is that the tank will be weathered along with the diorama groundwork, seamlessly joining the two together.

Adding metal wear marks to the tracks. Even when traversing dirty or muddy ground, the tank tracks would still have a metallic sheen. This is done with a 2B lead pencil. Note there is no join seam between the tank tracks and the groundwork.

important for the tank to sit without any daylight showing – it's bad form to have the tank 'hovering' on the diorama base. The excess Porion was blended into the existing groundwork with a wet brush. Once dry, this new area was blended by brushing PVA glue to the bare areas and sprinkling the same coloured grout as used on the rest of the base.

Now that the tank is secured to the base, it can be weathered. In previous chapters, I have described the weathering process in depth. This Marder was weathered the same way, except I used the grout from the groundwork to heavily dust the running gear. The running gear – wheels and tracks – was given a metallic sheen with a 2B pencil. The rest of the vehicle, especially the rear stowage basket and areas the crew worked in, were also weathered and chipped with the 2B pencil.

The other elements of the diorama, the knocked-out T-34 and the Schwimmwagen were weathered separately and joined to the base now. The T-34 I weathered to look like it had been blown up and burnt out. I started by painting it entirely with Tamiya XF1 Matt Black, and then applied two coats of Rustall. Rustall is incredible stuff, it literally rusts any surface. Care needs to be taken with Rustall, as it tends to eat Tamiya acrylic paint! The T-34 was then pastelled with a combination of rust and black pastels. As mentioned the Schwimmwagen was weathered using the same techniques as all the Marders, post shade, filter, pastels, and chips.

Finally, the figures can be glued to the base; I use Araldite two-part epoxy glue, for a really strong bond. Adding the figures to the base is the final step in this diorama, indeed the final step for the whole book.

None of the techniques described herein are revolutionary, merely methods I've seen used to great effect by other modellers, or others I've developed by trial and error. I feel the essence to modelling is having fun and experimentation; I hope that this guide to modelling Marders will encourage other modellers to have a go and attempt new methods.

RIGHT Rear of the Marder III Ausf. H. The colour of the groundwork has been brought up onto the vehicle. The tracks and areas of high wear have been seen to with the lead pencil. This Marder was weathered using all the techniques accumulated in the preceeding chapters.

BELOW MIG Productions destroyed T-34. This is an all-resin kit, complete with all the parts to build a wrecked vehicle. It's a great corner piece to the diorama, perfect for having the tank crew pose in front of for the camera.

ABOVE **The cameraman's Schwimmwagen. This little Tamiya kit is fantastic, it was built out of box, I added camera tripods and storage boxes to the back seats.**

BELOW AND NEXT PAGE **Views of the finished model.**

Gallery

THIS PAGE AND NEXT PAGE
Panzerjäger 38(t) für 7.62cm PaK36r – Marder III
Model by Pat Johnston. This Tamiya kit was detailed using Dragon models 'Grille' tracks, and Tamiya infantry gear, helmets, and water bottles. Pat painted the model with Tamiya acrylics, mixing his own shade using matt black and white. The vehicle markings are Archer dry transfers. Mud was applied to the vehicle before painting using sand, liquid glue and dried sage. Photos by Graeme Davidson.

Whitewashed Panzerjäger 38(t) mit 7.5cm PaK40/3 Ausf. M – Marder III Ausf. M
Model by Pat Johnston. This Tamiya kit was detailed using Tamiya's own turned-brass 7.5cm ammunition, designed specifically for this kit. Pat also added MIG Productions muzzle brake cover to the Tamiya gun barrel. The interior was detailed with fine fuse wire for all radio and intercom wiring, and various bits and pieces from the spares box. Pat used Tamiya acrylics to paint the model, using an Iwata Custom Micron Airbrush. Photos by Graeme Davidson.

7.5cm PaK40/1 auf Geschutzwagen Lorraine Schlepper(f), Sd.Kfz.135 – Marder I

Model by Gary Edmundson. This is an Alby all-resin kit. The kit comes with Tamiya's old PaK 40 gun, which Gary substituted with the gun from Tamiya's Marder III Ausf. M. Gary replaced the poor resin tracks with delicate Friulmodel white metal ones, and cast new road wheels from his own master. He detailed the kit with Aber tool brackets and Grandt Line rivets. The model was painted using Tamiya acrylics. He also applied a gloss varnish to take the decals, and finished it off with a coat of Testors' matt varnish. Photos by Gary Edmundson

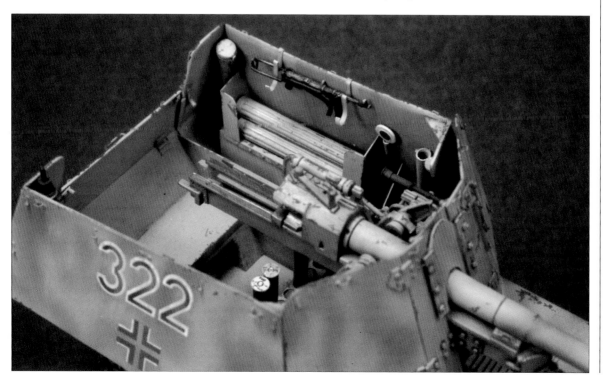

List of available kits and accessories

Manufacturer	Description	Type	Material	Vehicle
Alan Hobbies	Marder II Ausf. D	kit	plastic	Marder II Ausf. D
Ironside	Marder I	kit	resin, plastic, etch	Marder I
Italeri	Marder III Ausf. H	kit	plastic	Marder III Ausf. H
Tamiya	35225 Marder III Ausf. M	kit	plastic	Marder III Ausf. M
Tamiya	35248 Marder III auf Gw.38t	kit	plastic	Marder III
Tamiya	35258 Marder III Ausf. M projectiles	accessory	turned brass	Marder III Ausf. M
Aber	35L05 PaK 40/3 gun barrel	accessory	turned brass	Marder III Ausf. M
Aber	352054 TMD initial Marder III Ausf. M backdate	accessory	resin, leadfoil	Marder III Ausf. M
Aber	352055 TMD mid Marder III Ausf. M backdate	accessory	resin, leadfoil	Marder III Ausf. M
Aber	35100 Marder III detail	accessory	etch	Marder III
Aber	35101 fenders for Marder III	accessory	etch	Marder III
Aber	35125 detail for Marder III Ausf. M	accessory	etch	Marder III Ausf. M
Aber	35126 fenders for Marder III Ausf. M	accessory	etch	Marder III Ausf. M
Blast Models	BL35007K Update for Marder III Ausf. M	accessory	resin, turned brass	Marder III Ausf. M
Eduard	TP042 zoom set for Marder III Ausf. M	accessory	etch	Marder III Ausf. M
Eduard	TP043 PE detail for Marder III Ausf. M	accessory	etch	Marder III Ausf. M
Eduard	35528 details for Marder III Ausf. M	accessory	etch	Marder III Ausf. M
Eduard	35529 fenders for Marder III Ausf. M	accessory	etch	Marder III Ausf. M
Eduard	35266 details for Marder II	accessory	etch	Marder II Ausf. D
Eduard	35398 details for Marder III	accessory	etch	Marder III
Eduard	xt041 express mask for Marder III	accessory		Marder III
Friulmodellismo	ALT53 Marder II late workable track	accessory	white metal	Marder II Ausf. D
Friulmodellismo	Lorraine Schlepper track	accessory	white metal	Marder I
Jordi Rubio	35050 7.62cm Pak36(r) gun barrel	accessory	turned brass	Marder III
K59	replacement gun and details	accessory	resin, etch	Marder III Ausf. M
K59	replacement gun for Marder III	accessory	resin, etch	Marder III
K59	replacement upper armour for Marder III	accessory	resin, etch	Marder III
K59	replacement gun for Marder II	accessory	resin, etch	Marder II Ausf. D
MIG	35-015 winter tarp and muzzle cover	accessory	resin, vacform plastic	Marder III Ausf. M
ModelKasten	KA9 38t sprocket	accessory	plastic	Marder III
ModelKasten	SK30 38t track (workable)	accessory	plastic	Marder III
Modelkasten	SK56 tracks for Marder II Ausf. D	accessory	plastic	Marder II Ausf. D
Moskit	3532 Marder III Ausf. H metal exhaust	accessory	metal	Marder III Ausf. H
Part	35050 detail for Marder III	accessory	etch	Marder III
Part	35051 Marder III armour plate	accessory	etch	Marder III
Part	35052 Marder III fenders	accessory	etch	Marder III
Part	35053 Marder III shell rack	accessory	etch	Marder III
Royal Model	261 Marder III detail set	accessory	resin, etch	Marder III
Royal Model	298 Marder III Ausf. H details	accessory	resin, etch	Marder III Ausf. H
Royal Model	299 interior for Marder III Ausf. H	accessory	resin, etch	Marder III Ausf. H
Royal Model	300 Marder III Ausf. H details Pt2	accessory	resin, etch	Marder III Ausf. H
Royal Model	301 interior for Marder III	accessory	resin, etch	Marder III
Royal Model	311 Marder III Ausf. M interior detail.	accessory	resin, etch	Marder III Ausf. M
Royal Model	312 Marder III Ausf. M armour plate	accessory	etch	Marder III Ausf. M
WW2 Productions	35005 38t tracks (for all Marder IIIs)	accessory	resin	Marder III Ausf. M

Further reading

Books

The following is a list of books used throughout the planning, building and painting of the models contained within this book:

Andorfer, Block, Nelson et al, *Nuts & Bolts 15: Marder III*, 2001

Andorfer, Block, Nelson et al, *Nuts & Bolts 17: Marder III Ausf. M*, 2003

Andorfer, Block, Nelson et al, *Nuts & Bolts 18: Marder III Ausf. H*, 2004

Bitoh, Mitsuru, *Achtung Panzer 7: Pz.Kpfw I/II series and variants*, Model Graphix/Delta, 2003

Ichimura, Hihara, *Panzers at Saumur No. 3*, Model Graphix/Delta, 1992

Parada, Styrna, Jablonski, *Marder III*, Kagero, 1999

Perrett, Bryan, *New Vanguard 34: Sturmartillerie & Panzerjäger 1939–45*, Osprey, 1999

Scheibert, Horst, *Marder III*, Schiffer, 1998

Scheibert, Horst, *Panzerjäger*, Schiffer, 1994

Scheibert, Horst, *Panzerkampwagen 38(t)*, Schiffer, 1993

Thomas, Nigel, *Men-at-Arms 330: The German Army 1939–45 (4) Eastern Front*, Osprey, 1999

Thomas, Nigel, *Men-at-Arms 336: The German Army 1939–45 (5) Western Front*, Osprey, 2000

Windrow, Martin: *Men-at-Arms 24: The Panzer Divisions*, Osprey, 1982

Wydawnictwo Militaria 175 Marder III, Grille, Wydawnictwo, 1998

Wydawnictwo Militaria 209 Marder II, Wydawnictwo, 1998

Websites

As modellers we are lucky to have such a powerful research tool at our disposal – the internet. I do feel sometimes that the internet is a double-edged sword when it comes to modelling. Granted it's an incredible resource, but it's also a huge time waster! Here's a list of websites that I frequent.

- Missing Lynx: www.missing-lynx.com excellent general modelling website.
- Achtung Panzer: www.achtungpanzer.com contains information on all German World War II vehicles
- PMMS: www.perthmilitarymodelling.com a great site for kit reviews.
- Tamiya: www.tamiya.com

Here's the list of websites for the manufacturers that generously contributed to this book.

- Aber: http://www.aber.net.pl/
- Tiger Model Designs: http://www.tigermodels.com/
- Royal Models: http://www.royalmodel.com/
- CMK: http://www.cmkkits.com/
- Iwata airbrushes: www.arttalk.com/iwata/index

Museum vehicles

There is a large number of Marders of all marks stored in military museums around the world. Here is a listing of all the known Marders on display:

Marder I

- Saumur Musée des Blindés, Saumur, France. The vehicle is in excellent condition, as is much of the Saumur collection. Not on display to the public.

Marder II

(There are no surviving Marder II Ausf. D)

- Pansarimuseet Axvall, Sweden. Vehicle is in good condition externally, but most of the internal fittings are missing.
- Auto und Technick Museum Sinsheim, Germany. This is the ex-Aberdeen vehicle, and as such was exposed to the elements outside for much of its life. Vehicle in poor condition, but I believe it to be on loan to be restored.

Marder III

- Aberdeen Proving Ground, Maryland, USA. Vehicle captured in North Africa, stored on outside display for 60 years. Slowly rusting away.
- Saumur Musée des Blindés, Saumur, France.

Marder III Ausf. H

- Auto und Technick Museum Sinsheim, Germany. Ex-WTS Koblenz, Germany. Vehicle in good condition.
- Henriquez Collection, Trieste, Italy.

Marder III Ausf. M

- Aberdeen Proving Ground, Maryland, USA. Late-production Marder III Ausf. M, recognisable by the welded driver's hood. Unfortunately like much of Aberdeen's collection, quietly rusting away on outside display.
- Saumur Musée des Blindés, Saumur, France. Late-production Marder III Ausf. M. Good condition, and a rare one in that it appears to be a command vehicle, fitted with extra radios
- Victory Museum, Arlon, Belgium. Cobbled together from a regular Panzer 38t. Not a real Marder at all.
- Henriquez Collection, Trieste, Italy. Early model Marder III Ausf. M with cast driver's hood.

Index